AF674005

Ujjain

✷ *Lingam of Mahakala with Shringaras*

Ujjain
The City of Temples

M.K. Pal

NIYOGI BOOKS

Published by
NIYOGI BOOKS
D-78, Okhla Industrial Area, Phase-I
New Delhi-110 020, INDIA
Tel: 91-11-26816301, 49327000
Fax: 91-11-26810483, 26813830
Email: niyogibooks@gmail.com
Website: www.niyogibooksindia.com

Editor: P.K. Jayanthan
Design: Nabanita Das

ISBN: 978-93-83098-51-4
Publication: 2014

Printed at: Niyogi Offset Pvt. Ltd., New Delhi, India

Dedicated to
Shri K.N. Dikshit, a distinguished
author and a doyen of Indian
archaeologists

Contents

✷ *Mahakaleshwar Temple during night*

Page 6-7: *Mahakaleshwar Temple*

Foreword

This book titled *Ujjain: The City of Temples* by Dr M.K. Pal is intended to provide important and helpful information to the English-knowing inter-state visitors and foreign tourists who would like to have a glimpse of the various aspects of the age old temple culture of Ujjain, a city of temples located in the heart of India. The book basically records the salient features of the temple culture of Ujjain with special emphasis on their historical and socio-cultural perspectives. To make the book more interesting to its readers, the author has nicely interwoven his document with anecdotes and legends associated with the centres of worship. The architectural details and rituals of the temples have also been depicted by the author in a succinct and coherent manner. This work is the outcome of Dr Pal's painstaking research and in-depth study based on field investigations. He has tried to cover most of the Brahmanical religious shrines in Ujjain and enhanced the quality of the book with sharp and beautiful illustrations.

As one of the renowned Hindu places of pilgrimage in India, Ujjain is always visited by a huge number of pilgrims and visitors from all over India, especially from the neighbouring states of Uttar Pradesh, Rajasthan, Gujarat, and Maharashtra. The book will automatically draw the attention of a varied class of readers including those who are seriously interested to carry on further research on the temple culture of Ujjain. A must have for those who are eager to know more about the great poet Kālidāsa's Ujjain, the blissful land of gods.

12/5/14

B.R. Mani
Additional Director General
Archaeological Survey of India
Ministry of Culture
New Delhi

Introduction

Temples have always played an important role in the socio-cultural life of the people. There is no denying the fact that temple became an aesthetic formulation of an essentially theistic religion. Through it, men sought to make all that their beliefs symbolised accessible to their sense-perception. These beliefs indeed influenced and commanded individuals in the privacy of their conscience. But as a visible emblem of the religion, philosophy, and ethics of the people, temple played a significant role far more vital than any other institution. It became a symbol of dharma for all. The architecture of temples only conveyed in spatial terms the intensity of the peoples' longing for a 'life of relief'. The God or Goddess to whom the structure was dedicated symbolised the Supreme Principle which controlled the affairs of the world, and directed the spiritual urge.

Due to this, the temple became the centre of all civic and social activities in the ancient city of Ujjain. The temple structures dominated the surroundings by their location as well as size. As a matter of fact, the temples functioned as the preserver of traditional values. Every locality grew around a temple which was the hub of activities.

Even today, the daily rituals in temples give assured employment to a group of people such as the priests, Brahmins, musicians, florists, and other functionaries. A temple festival is an occasion of great social rejoicing. People from surrounding villages gather to participate in the general merriment. These festivals generally end up as fairs, often lasting several days. Merchants and petty traders from places far and near arrive to barter or sell goods. To the devotees, the temples are spots of admiration being the abode of the Gods or *devasthan*. The evolution of temple architecture from its simple unostentatious beginnings into an agglomeration of large and complicated structures perhaps conforms to the growing emotional demands of the devotees.

It is presumed that river Shipra (also known as Kshipra) has undoubtedly earned the distinction of establishing a pattern of temple culture in Ujjain which has persisted to this day. A visit to the temples of this holy city, situated on the right bank of Shipra, is still considered a pilgrimage. As a religious centre, Ujjain is as important as Varanasi, Gaya, and Kanchi. Shaivism, Vaishnavism, and their various cults and sects, as well as Jainism and Buddhism, have found a niche in this age-old catholic city. Avanti Khanda of the *Skanda Purana* mentions innumerable temples dedicated to Shakti and her various forms. The Siddha and the Natha cults,

✷ *Inner view of Dwarakadhish Gopal temple*

offshoots of tantricism, also flourished in this holy city. Even today the temples are considered means for peace, happiness, and salvation. A visit to the temples of Ujjain reveals their fundamental role linking the world of Gods to the people of the area where they are located.

It is difficult to trace the period of origin and growth of temple culture in Ujjain. Ujjain is more than 5,000 years old. While the city's early history is lost in the midst of antiquity, by the 6th century BCE, Avanti, with its capital Ujjain, is mentioned in the Buddhist literature as one of the four greatest powers, the others being Vatsya, Kosala, and Magadha. Ujjain is one of the 51 Shaktipeethas. The *Skanda Purana* mentions that 84 Mahadevas, 64 Yoginis, eight Bhairavas, and six Vinayakas (Ganeshas) exist there.

It is believed that once a majestic Sun Temple existed in Ujjain. Avanti Mahatmya of *Skanda Purana* describes the Sun Temple and two pools named Surya Kund and Brahma Kund. People from nearby villages take ritual dip in Surya Kund even today. Remains of the old temple are scattered all over the area. As it appears, Ujjain was developed as a sacred place in the ancient kingdom of western Malwa. According to S.M. Bhardwaj, it may never be known whether it was developed at the site of a former cult spot of the pre-Aryans. But the fact remains that its location on the trunk root from the Ganga plain to the Arabian Sea may have made it a centre for pilgrimage as well as trade. Archaeologists agree that the impetus for the growth of Ujjain came from the iron using culture of the Gangetic plains. At about 500 BCE Ujjain thus lay, in the epic context, 'on a main highway of the southward-intruding Aryan culture' (Bhardwaj 1973: p. 39. See also Wheeler 1968: page 142).

It may thus be assumed that Ujjain, also known as Ujjayini or Avanti, historically, emerged as the first major centre for commercial and cultural activities in the Malwa region during India's second wave of urbanisation in the 7th century BCE, the first being the Indus Valley Civilisation. Around 600 BCE an earthen rampart was built around Avanti, a city of considerable size. Avanti was one of the prominent Mahajanapadas of the Indo-Aryans. In the post-Mahabharata period around 500 BCE Avanti was a prominent kingdom in western India. It was ruled by the Haihayas, who were possibly of mixed Indo-Aryan and aboriginal origin.

The temple culture of Ujjain is deemed to be the agglomeration of a pattern of culture that developed through a process of spontaneous revelations of the following basic units of cultural exponents:

* historical perspectives
* temples and their respective cult associations
* daily schedule including *puja* and other ritual performances / offerings
* traditional beliefs, myths, and legends connected with the temple
* fairs and festivals
* temple artifacts including ritual utensils
* temple architecture
* temple economy
* temple administration including the role of the priest
* community service
* pilgrimage and eco-friendly tourism

Historical Perspectives

History of the ancient town of Ujjain is interwoven with legends. According to one legend, Shiva, the destroyer of the universe, descended from heaven to Mrityulok, the land of mortals, to get rid of Ujjain's demon king Tripura. Another legend has it that this ancient town got its name when king Shiva of Avanti commemorated his victory over the demon ruler of Tripura by renaming his capital Avantipura as Ujjayini (one who conquers with pride). It is also said that the blue god Krishna came to Sandipani Muni Ashram in Ujjain, to study under the great sage, Sandipani Muni.

Myths apart, Ujjayini (now Ujjain), the capital of King Pradyota of Avanti, situated on the eastern bank of Shipra, was more than a mere metropolis or even a centre of learning. Ujjaini was referred to as Ozene by Ptolemy. *Periplus of the Erythrean Sea* is the account of an unknown Greek merchant, then residing in

Egypt, who made a voyage to India sometime in the 2nd half of the 1st century CE. The Periplus talks of Ozene (Ujjain) in the east of Barygaza (Brigukachachha, now Broach), which imported items like Onyx, Porcelain, fine Muslins, Spikenard, and cast godellium to this important region of India. Articles such as precious stones and pearls, scents, spices, perfumes, silks, muslin, etc. reached the port of Brigukachachha for export to the western world from the remote north through Ujjain, connected by land route.

Ujjain has also been the first meridian of longitude for the Hindu Geographers since 4th century BCE. As per *Mahabharata*, Ujjayini was the capital of Avanti. Ashoka, who subsequently became the emperor, is said to have resided in the city when he was the viceroy of the western provinces of the Maurya empire. While Ashoka was the emperor of Magadha, a Buddhist monastery existed in Ujjain. Inscriptions of Bhoja, Udayaditya, Naravarman, Devapaldeo, and Vijayasinghadeva have been discovered from Ujjain. During their reign Mahakaleshwar temple was also a seat of Sanskrit learning. Several important Jain temples, too, existed there during those days.

Ujjain was also ruled by the Sungas and the Satavahanas in the post-Mauryan period. Nasik cave inscription of Usavadatta mentions that a hundred thousand Brahmins dined through the charity of Usavadatta in 'Ujeni' city. The votive inscription of Sanchi also refers to the donor from Ujeni. Some inhabitants of Ujjaini are also mentioned in the Nagarjunikonda pillar inscription. The Satavahanas and the Indo-scythian Sakas contested for the possession of the city for a long period. Following the end of Satavahana dynasty, the city was ruled by the

Sakas from the 2nd to the 4th century CE. After the conquest over Sakas by the Guptas, Ujjayini became part of the Gupta empire. The city soon gained prominence and became an important seat in the annals of that empire.

Vikramaditya of Kalidasa is supposed to be Chandragupta II. His famous court in Ujjain was noted for the presence of celebrated poets and scholars, including Kalidasa, the celebrated author of the immortal drama *Abhigyana Shakuntalam.* As a poet, Kalidasa was not impervious to Ujjain's beauty. In *Meghadutam* the poet's love for Ujjain finds full expression. The poet describes the imaginary passage of clouds over Ujjaini. It is almost as if it loaths to move on, for in 12 verses (27–38), there is a lyrical description of the city and the people who conjure up a vivid picture of a civilised attractive society, a leisured class and yet imbued with deeply religious pre-occupations.

Another Sanskrit scholar and poet felt that Ujjain was 'the very home of the golden age; paved with jewels, full of romance with dancing girls in the temples and love in everyone's hearts'. Around 500 CE, Malwa re-emerged from the dilapidated Gupta empire as a separate kingdom. In 528 CE Yasodharman of Malwa defeated the Hunas, who had invaded India from the north-west. During the 7th century CE, the region became part of Harsha's empire, who disputed the region with Chalukya king Pulakesin II of Badami in the Deccan.

Ujjain has been a holy place for the Hindus. The Buddhists and the Jains also linked Avanti with Sramana leaders. Under Mahakachhayana, who was born in the city, Buddhism spread throughout Avanti. Mahavira, the Jain Tirthankara, is said to have performed penances in Avanti and its capital where he refused to be dissuaded. It is also associated with the Lingayats. When the Chinese pilgrim Hiuen Tsang visited this place, its boundary was 30 li (5 miles). The kingdom of Ujjain was under the rule of a Brahmin Raja. Then there were three or four monasteries in fairly good condition, providing shelter to about 300 monks. There were numerous temples. In fact Hinduism, Buddhism, and Jainism co-existed peacefully in Ujjain for a long time.

Later Ujjain came under the political sway of the Kalachuris, the Maitrakas, the later Guptas, the Pushyabhutis, the Pratiharas, and the Rashtrakutas. Ultimately in the latter part of the 10th century CE the Paramaras of Malwa overthrew the yoke of their Rashtrakuta overlords and attained freedom. Siyaka II, Vakpati Munja, Sindhuraja, Bhojadeva, Udayaditya, and Naravarman had been the Paramara rulers of Malwa, and Ujjaini and Dhar were the capitals. These rulers, particularly Bhoja, had been patrons of literature, arts, and architecture.

The power of the Paramaras crumbled in front of Muslim invasions. During the invasion of Ujjain in 1235 CE, Delhi Sultan Iltutmish led the destruction of the great shrine of Mahakala and other religious and cultural centres of Ujjain. After the Khilji invasion of Malwa in the 1st decade of the 14th century CE the Paramara power was finally extinguished in 1401 CE. Ujjain then passed on to the hands of the Muslims.

Fortunately, in the beginning of the 17th century CE both Ujjain and Malwa were ruled by the Marathas under the Peshwas who controlled the entire area. The Maratha domination gave impetus

✷ *Ram Ghat on the banks of Shipra river*

to a culture/temple building. Modern Ujjain thus came into being. The Mahakaleshwar and Harsiddhi temples were reconstructed during this period. Gopal Mandir in the main market too was constructed then. Ujjain finally passed on to the hands of the Scindias in 1750 CE. It was their main centre until 1810 CE when they shifted to Gwalior.

Today a large number of temples exist in Ujjain. Though built on old sites, most of them have been recently constructed. Modern Ujjain is a striking amalgamation of legacy of the bygone era and modernity of contemporary architecture. Though the structure of the temples are more recent, the temples form an integral part of the city's infrastructure and contribute to the continuity of Ujjain's age-old tradition of greatness.

Ujjain has a long history. History of about 2000 years is known from the literature and archaeological remains. Renowned as a centre of learning as well as astronomical and mathematical research; home to the cultural heritage of Hinduism, Buddhism, and Jainism; seat of the mighty rulers from Prodyata to Paramaras; the centre for exporting precious and semi-precious stones to the western world; Ujjayini served the multiple purposes of catering to interests in the political, cultural, and economic fields. Its location was very convenient to act as a link between the north and the south-west, and through it followed ideas and goods from one part of India to the other.

Temples and Their Cultic Associations

Hindu temples and places of pilgrimage are symbols of religious belief. They reflect the vitality, resilience, and syncretism. They broadly define and continually re-emphasise the Hindu sacred space. They knit together the linguistically diverse Hindu population socially, culturally, and spatically at different integrative levels. Their significance is to be measured from their capacity to generate and maintain a massive system of religious beliefs.

An important place of pilgrimage and popular holy city of temples, Ujjain is widely known as the land of Gods. This sacred city, situated on the banks of the sacred river Shipra, has played a significant role in the propagation of traditional as well as reinterpreted religious beliefs through the ages. Ujjain abounds in temples, with hoary traditions attached to each. The number of temples in Ujjain is so large that, it is popularly believed that if one comes with two cartloads of grain and offers one handful at each temple, one would still run short of the grain. But considering the antiquity, popularity, and its socio-cultural role in the society, the following ten temples have been chosen for discussion in this book. It is expected that the data on these temples would throw more light on hitherto unknown facts on the temple culture of Ujjain, considered by Hindus as one of the seven sacred cities.

1. Mahakaleshwar temple
2. Kalabhairava temple
3. Chintaman Ganesha temple
4. Gadkalika temple
5. Gopal mandir
6. Mangalnath temple
7. Harsiddhi temple
8. Bade Ganeshji temple
9. Navagraha temple
10. Sandipani ashram

Mahakaleshwar Temple

Mahakaleshwar temple is considered to be one of the most renowned Shiva temples in India. One of the 12 celebrated *Jyotirlingas* has been consecrated here. The glory of the temple has been vividly described in various puranas. Starting with the great Kalidasa, many other Sanskrit poets have also eulogised this temple in emotive terms. The presiding deity of time, Shiva, in all His splendour, reigns eternal in Ujjain. As the distinctive presiding deity of Ujjain, Mahakaleshwar dominates the life of the city and its people even in the midst of the busy modern preoccupations and provides an unbreakable link with age-old traditions. The *Lingam* at the temple is believed to be *swayambhu* (self-manifested), deriving currents of power (*shakti*) from itself as against the other images and *Lingams* which are ritually consecrated and invested with the power of *mantra*. The idol of Mahakaleshwar is known as Dakshinamurti, or one who is facing the south. This is a unique feature, upheld by tantric tradition, found only here among the 12 *Jyotirlingas*.

✷ *Three storeyed temple of Mahakaleshwar*

It deserves mention in this context that the images of Shiva in his terrific (*ugra*) forms as Aghora, Bhairava, and Mahakala have bulging eyes, inflated cheeks, tusks, etc. The basic structure of these faces is that of man whereas it is that of the lion in the image of Shiva as Sarabhesa. The idol of Omkareshwar Shiva is consecrated in the sanctum above the Mahakaleshwar shrine. The images of Ganesha, Parvati, and Kartikeya are installed in the west, north, and east of the *garbhagriha*, respectively. On the south stands the image of Nandi. The idol of Nagchandreshwar on the third storey is open for *darshan* only on *Nagpanchami*. During Mahashivaratri a huge fair is held in the temple complex and the worship continues throughout the night.

It is very difficult to say when Mahakaleshwar temple came into existence. According to a story, a powerful demon that lived on Ratnamal mountain attacked Avanti (now Ujjain) and killed a Brahmin sage by throwing him into fire. The angry Lord Shiva opened his third eye and burnt the demon to ashes. The *Shivalingam* (symbolic phallus of Shiva) appeared at that

✷ *Lingam of Mahakala with different Shringaras done in the month of Phalgun*

very spot. A majestic temple was built there. The mention of this temple is also found in *Adi Brahma Purana* and its detailed description in the *Gyansamhita.*

When the illustrious king Vikramaditya ruled Ujjaini, he used to visit Mahakaleshwar temple every day. He used to bow before the Shivalingam in all humility and prayed to Lord Shiva mercifully to grant prosperity and happiness to his subjects and peace to the land over which he ruled. He also used to place 111 *bel* leaves one by one on the Shivalingam, praising Lord Shiva by reciting suitable eulogies.

In the 6th century BCE King Chandra Pradyota appointed prince Kumarasena to look after the law and order situation of the Mahakaleshwar temple. It deserves special mention that Lord Shiva in human form was found on Ujjain coins of circa 3rd to 2nd century BCE (Catalogue of Coins of Ancient India in the British Museum, London, 1936, p. 85, pl. XI, no. 2).

Kalidasa in his *Raghuvamsam* has described Mahakaleshwar temple as 'niketana', which probably indicates that the roof of the temple was flat, and there was no *shikhara* on the temple. In the initial portion of *Meghadutam* (Purva Megha), Kalidasa gives a fascinating description of Mahakaleshwar temple. It appears that the temple might have been a unique example of the art and architecture prevailing then. The temple was enclosed by high ramparts attached with the entry gates. At twilight the lively rows of glittering lamps lighted up the temple complex. The whole atmosphere echoed with the sound of various musical instruments. The well-decorated damsels added a lot to the

✷ *A panoramic view of the Mahakaleshwar Temple*

aesthetic beauty of the temple. The assembly of the devotees in large numbers in the temple was indicative of its popularity and its religious and socio-cultural role in the society.

After the downfall of the Gupta empire, several dynasties, such as Maitrakas, Chalukyas, later Guptas, Kalachuris, Pushyabhutis, Gurjara Pratiharas, and Rashtrakutas, dominated the political scene in Ujjain. During this period a number of temples of various gods and goddesses as well as other religious establishments came up in Avanti. Several Shaivaite temples, including those of the 84 Mahadevas, existed here. But the development and progress of Mahakaleshwar temple and its religio-cultural milieu always remained important. All the ruling dynasties unhesitatingly distributed endowments to this temple. The glamour and significance of the temple is also reflected in the contemporary poetical works such as *Harshacharita* and *Kadambari* of Banabhatta, *Naishadhacharita* of Shri Harsha and *Navasahasanka Charita* of Padmagupta.

During 9th to 12th century CE the Paramaras became so identified with Ujjain that subsequent tradition converted Vikramaditya to a Paramara. A contemporary inscription testifies that Mahakaleshwar temple was rebuilt during the reign of Udayaditya and Naravarman during the 11th and 12th centuries CE. It was built in the Paramaras' favourite Bhumija style of architecture. Remains available in the temple complex and the neighbouring places authenticate this fact. The Bhumija mode of temples bears unique artistic features in plan and elevation. The artisans adopted the classical approach in the schemes of the temples. Perhaps the Malwan text *Samarangana*, and then *Aparajita* had deeply impacted the minds of the people and their patrons. The temples of this style had either *triratha* or *pancharatha* in their plans.

The main features of these temples were their shape like a star and the *shikhara*. So far as the *shikhara* is concerned, *urusrngas* (mini spires) generally of odd numbers, with gradually decreasing number of rows between the well decorated spines (*haravali* or *lata*) rose up at the cardinal points from *chaityas* and *sukanasas* ultimately surmounted by *amalaka*. The temple was glutted with decorative motifs or images all over. Horizontally, the shrine was divided from front to back in entrance, *ardhamandapa* sanctum, *antarala* (vestibule), *garbhagriha* and *pradakshinapatha.* Upper components of the temple rested on the strong and well-designed pillars and pilasters. Such temples, according to the contemporary architectural science contained the images of various gods and goddesses, *Navagrahas* (nine planets), Apsaras (celestial dancers), female dancers, *anucharas* (attendants), *kichakas*, and so on. The sculptural art of the temple had been very classical and multifarious. Shaivite images of Nataraja, Kalyanasundara, Ravananugraha, Gajantaka, Sadashiva, Andhakasura-slayer, Lakulisha, and so on were installed in the temples. The temples were also adorned with images of Ganesha, Parvati, Brahma, Vishnu, Surya (Sun god), *Saptamatrikas* (seven mother goddesses), and so on. These images were very proportionate, well decorated, sculpturally perfect, and carved according to classical and puranic methods. The worships and the conduct of rituals continued in some way or the other. *Prabhandha Chintamani, Vividha Tritha Kalpataru,* and *Prabhandha Kosha,* all composed during 13th–14th century CE, reveal this. Similarly mention is also made in *Vikramacharita* and *Bhojacharita* composed in the 15th century CE. According to the epic *Hammira Mahakavya*, Hammira, the ruler of Ranathombhor worshipped lord Mahakaleshwar during his stay in Ujjain.

When Paramara king Siladitya was defeated by the Sultans of Mandu, Ujjain passed on to the hands of the Muslims. Thus began a long era of misfortune and decay. The ancient glory of Ujjain was marred by repeated inroads of attacking hordes. The invasion of Ujjain in 1234 CE by Iltutmish, the second Slave king triggered off systematic desecration and despoiling of temples. In 1305 CE, Allaudin Khalji, the powerful ruler of the Khalji dynasty of the

Delhi Sultanate, captured Ujjain. Muhammad-bin-Tughlaq, the second ruler of the Tughlaq dynasty, attacked Central India. For a short while Ujjain was ruled by the Afghan Sur dynasty under Shujjat Khan and his son Buz Bahadur who was finally defeated by the Mughal Emperor Akbar in 1562 CE. Akbar succeeded in subduing most of the regional rulers. He constructed a city wall for the defence of Ujjain.

A few *sanads* (written instructions or orders) issued by the then Mughal rulers testify that during the medieval period some of the Islamic rulers, including Emperor Aurangzeb, contributed financially to preserve the glory of Ujjain's ancient temples, and they also respected Mahakaleshwar temple. This was obviously done for the safety of their reign.

At the beginning of 17th century CE Ujjain underwent another period of invasions at the hands of Marathas, who gradually captured the entire region. In the 4th decade of 18th century CE Maratha regime was established in Ujjain. The administration of Ujjain was assigned by Peshwa Bajirao I to his faithful commander Ranoji Scindia, the founder of the ruling house of Gwalior. The Dewan of Ranoji was Sukhtankar Ramchandra Baba Shenvi, a wealthy but issueless Brahmin. On the suggestion of Pandits and well-wishers, he reconstructed the famous Mahakaleshwar temple in Ujjain during the 4th–5th decades of 18th century CE.

The present temple has three storeys. *Lingam*s of Mahakaleshwar, Omkareshwar, and Nagachandreshwar (worshipped in the form of Shivalinga) are installed in the lower, middle, and upper storeys, respectively. Omkareshwar Mahadeva here is looked after by the

Dashnami sadhus of the Mahanirvan order. It is considered to be the *pratirupa* (image) of Omkareshwara Jyotirlinga situated on the banks of river Narmada.

There is a large *kund* (pool) named Koti tirtha (water source of Mahakaleshwar temple premises) in the temple complex. The *kund* has been built in the sarvatobhadra style. On the path adjoining the stairs of the *kund*, one can see several images representing the sculptural grandeur of the temple built during the Paramara period. In the east of the *kund* is a large verandah which has an entrance to the path leading to the *garbhagriha.*

Lord Mahakala, Ganesha, Parvati, and Kartikeya are seated here in sequence. In the *garbhagriha* there are two *akhanda jyotis*. It is said that emperor Aurangzeb had issued a *sanad* to provide for the expenses of ghee for these lamps. In the *sabhagriha* outside, the statue of Nandi, Shiva's bull, can be seen. The statue has been silver plated a few years ago.

In the northern side of the verandah, the images of Sri Rama and Goddess Avantika are worshipped. In the southern side of the main shrine, many miniature Shaivite temples built during the Shinde regime can be seen. Among them the temples of Vriddha Mahakaleshwar, Anadi Kalpeshwar, and Saptarshi are prominent and represent outstanding examples of architecture.

The Lingam of Mahakaleshwar is colossal. The silver-plated Naga Jaladhari and the inscribed and esoteric silver plate covering the roof of the *garbhagriha* add extra grandeur to the shrine. Classical eulogies in the praise of Lord Shiva are exhibited all round the walls. The *akhanda jyoti* continuously burn. At the exit a very attractive metal sculpture of Nandi can be seen in a hall. Adjoining to this temple, there are two pillared projections facing the east and adding a lot to the architecture of the temple. The temple of Mahakaleshwar is a planned admixture of Bhumija, Chalukya, and Maratha styles of architecture. The *shikhara* with mini *sringas* is very peculiar. It may be noted here that during the past few years the upper portion of the *shikhara* has been plated with gold. It is also noteworthy that the storeys of the temple are ornamented with pierced balustrades, and the balconies have richly decorated roofs reminiscent of the Rajput style of architecture. Screens and pavilions are combined with marble colonnades leading to the Linga within the sanctuary, making Mughal architecture come alive right at the heart of this Hindu temple. The Mahakaleshwar temple is indeed a cherished site and a sculputural delight as well.

As noted earlier, the present temple of Mahakaleshwar was built betwen 4th and 5th decades of the 18th century CE. Simultaneously, the religious-minded Maratha nobles also built a number of temples in the Mahakaleshwar temple complex. During this period many ancient traditions such as *abhisheka*, *arati*, *sawari* (procession in the month of Sravana), Harihara milan, and so on were also revived. These traditions are undertaken even now with great enthusiasm. The Bhasma Aarti in early morning, Mahashivaratri, Panchakrosi yatra, Somavati Amavasya, and so on are special religious occasions interwoven with the rituals of the temple. Proper repairs and maintenance of the temple complex is done at the time of Kumbha Mela. A separate 'mandapam' was constructed in 1980 for visitors. In 1992, Madhya Pradesh government and Ujjain Development

Authority undertook repairs and maintenance and made provisions for the stay of pilgrims. The process is also followed during other important fairs and festivals.

The architecture of Mahakaleshwar temple and the underlying spirit in it need not only to be different from ordinary buildings and houses, but has also to dominate its surroundings. The upward thrust of the sanctum tower is symbolic of its spiritual eminence. The tower loudly announces the presence of Mahakaleshwar. At close range the temple overwhelms the faithful by the variety and wealth of exquisite carvings and architecture on its walls, pillars, and ceilings. The temple itself is an enormous piece of sculpture and its architectural features are often proof of the carvers' skill. Figures of various gods and goddesses, floral motifs, miniature Shaiva temples, exhibition of classical eulogies all round the walls in the praise of Lord Shiva, figure of metal-coated Nandi, and silver-plated Jaladhari – all are meant to reveal the righteous ways of the God to the believer. In short, the religious faith that the architecture of the temple evokes does not spring from a cynical denial of life, but from its warmest depths. In the presentation of this idea the architect was willing to be governed by established conventions rather than his inventive genius. The architecture of Mahakaleshwar temple is only sought to convey, in spatial terms, the intensity of its builders' longing to identify the divine with the real.

The Mahakaleshwar temple has been described as the Vaikuntha on the earth. The temple complex houses a number of other mini temples dedicated to other gods and goddesses. Mahakaleshwar is unique with a number of smaller temples on its premises. No

19th century CE. Previously when the temple did not have the entrance from the corridors, devotees used to take darshan of Ganesha at this temple before entering the *garbhagriha* of Mahakaleshwar temple.

Sakshi Gopal Temple

Sakshi Gopal temple is located near the Riddhi–Siddhi Vinayaka temple. It is believed that after praying at Mahakaleshwar temple, Gopalji's darshan should be taken as He provides the *sakshi* (evidence) of the darshan of the devotee, when Mahadeva wakes up from the *samadhi.*

Sankatmochan Siddhadas Hanuman Temple

Sankatmochan Siddhadas Hanuman temple, located in the north-west direction of Mahakaleshwar temple, was built by Samartha Ramdas, the Guru of Chhtrapati Shivaji. A large number of devotees throng this temple on Tuesdays and Saturdays.

Svapneshwara Mahadeva Temple

Located opposite to Sankatmochan Hanuman temple, Svapneshwara Mahadeva Temple is one of the 84 Mahadeva temples of the city of Ujjain. According to *Skanda Purana*, darshan of this Mahadeva helps one not to see evil dreams. Special pujas are offered on the 8th and 14th days of the fortnight.

Brihaspateshwara Mahadeva Temple

Brihaspateshwara Mahadeva temple is located at the north of the Svapneshwara Mahadeva temple. Brihaspati is worshipped here in the form of a Shivalinga. On every Thursday the deity is worshipped with yellow puja items.

Trivishtapeshwara Mahadeva Temple

Trivishtapeshwara Mahadeva temple is an ancient Shiva temple situated behind the Mahakaleshwar temple. This is one of the famed 84 Mahadeva temples. An adjacent chamber to this temple holds 11 Shivalingas.

Navagraha Temple

The Navagraha temple is situated near the exit gate of the Mahakaleshwar temple. The nine planets are represented here by nine Shivalingas.

Marutinandan Hanuman Temple

Marutinandan Hanuman temple is about 200 years old. The temple is situated under a huge pipal tree in the north-south direction of the Mahakaleshwar temple complex.

Neelakantheshwara Temple

Neelakantheshwara temple is situated behind the exit gate of Mahakaleshwar temple. Lord Neelakantheshwara is worshipped in order to relieve the world from its sufferings. As per *Srimad Bhagvata Mahapurana* Lord Shiva drank the halahala poison emerged during *samudramanthana* (ocean churning) and caused to stick it in his throat which turned his throat into blue. He, thus, came to be known as Neelakantheshwara (the one with a blue neck).

Khanderao Temple

Khanderao temple is situated near Neelakantheswara temple. Built by the king of Dewas, the temple is dedicated to Khanderao, the famous deity of Maharashtra. Special puja is offered on the Champashasthi day every year.

Govindeshwara Mahadeva Temple

Govindeshwara Mahadeva temple is in front of Juna Mahakaleshwar.

Suryamukhi Hanuman Temple

Suryamukhi Hanuman temple is situated near the main entrance of Mahkaleshwar temple on the *pradakshina path* (circumambulatory passage) of Koti tirtha.

Lakshmi Pradata Modh Ganesha Temple

Lakshmi Pradata Modh Ganesha temple is situated at the north of Koti tirtha. Offering puja at this temple before marriage or starting a new business, etc. is considered to be very auspicious. On Wednesdays and during Chaturthi, special puja is performed here. This is one of the city's famous six Vinayaka temples.

Svarnajaleshwara Mahadeva Temple

Svarnajaleshwara Mahadeva temple belongs to one of the 84 Mahadeva temples. Worship of this deity fulfils wishes.

Shani Temple

Shani temple is located in the north-east of the Koti tirtha.

Koteshwara Mahadeva Temple

Koteshwara, one of the *Ganas* of Lord Mahakaleshwar, is the presiding deity of Koti tirtha. On *pradosh* day Koteshwara is worshipped before the evening worship of Mahakaleshwar.

Saptarshi Temple

In the backward of Mahakaleswar temple there are seven temples dedicated to the seven *rishis* (seers). Rishi Panchami is observed on the 5th day of the Bhadrapada bright fortnight. Women offer puja to the *saptarshis* at these temples on this day. On the occasion of rakshabandhan, Brahmins offer puja to their ancestor *rishis*.

Anadikalpeshwara Mahadeva Temple

Anadikalpeshwara Mahadeva temple is situated opposite to *saptarshi* temple complex. Anadikalpeshwara temple is also one of the 84 Mahadeva temples. According to *Skanda Purana*, in the beginning of the world a quarrel took place between Brahma and Vishnu as both wanted to take credit for creation. A divine voice asked them to search for the end of Anadikalpeshwara Linga in Mahakala forest. On finding the linga, Brahma went to the top and Vishnu to the bottom. Having failed to find the end, Vishnu returned. He accepted his defeat. Brahma too could not find the end but lied that he did. Cow and *kewda* were his fake witnesses. Enraged by Brahma's lie, Shiva cut one of his four heads. Shiva cursed the cow that its mouth will always touch filth and *kewda* flower was prohibited from Shiva puja.

Sri Bal Vijay Mast Hanuman Temple

Lord Hanuman was known as Bal Vijay Mast Hanuman in his childhood. On Hanuman Ashtami and Hanuman Jayanti, *abhishek* and special pujas are offered at Sri Bal Vijay Mast Hanuman temple. Vermillion is offered to the deity and beautiful *shringara* done on Tuesdays and Saturdays.

Omkareshwara Mahadeva Temple

Omkareshwara Mahadeva temple is another Mahadeva temple in the Mahakaleshwar temple complex.

Vruddhakaleshwara Mahakala Temple

It is believed that the Shivalinga at Vruddhakaleshwara Mahakala temple is of one of the Shiva *ganas*. Before darshan of the Jyotirlinga in the Mahakaleshwar temple, darshan of this Shiva *gana* is undertaken.

Apart from the temples, several idols have been kept in the Mahakaleshwar temple complex. For example, there are 11 ancient Shivalingas in a chamber adjacent to the Trivishtapeshwara temple. On the walls many ancient Shiva-Parvati idols have been kept. On every *ekadashi*, 11th day of the Lunar fortnight, devotees offer puja here. The Naagbandha inscription, dated 11th century C.E., can be seen behind the Mahakaleshwar temple. This is a praise of Mahakaleshwar temple.

The Ganesha idol above the silver gate of the temple also deserves to be mentioned. Pilgrims offer flowers here before entering the temple. In a chamber on the north of Omkareshwara temple a beautiful idol of goddess Bhadrakali can be seen. In the north-south direction of the premises a *vriksha triveni*, or grove consisting of *vata, pipal* and *neem* is seen. It is believed that worshipping this grove yields merits equivalent to those of bathing in Triveni (confluence of the three sacred rivers, Ganges, Yamuna, and Saraswati). Below the Triveni and behind the Marutinandan Hanuman temple, a beautiful but small Sri Ram temple has been built.

Ujjain's temple culture is manifested in the sacred Koti tirtha. According to the puranas, the pool contains waters of all sacred rivers of India. The *tirtha* is also referred to in the Mahabharata.

Bhima, son of Pandu, after taking a dip in this *tirtha*, had darshan of Bhootbhavana. *Abhishek* of Mahakaleshwar is performed daily with water from this *tirtha*. Pandits sing the glory of Lord Mahakaleshwar sitting on the stairs of this *tirtha*.

Daily Pujas (Worships) and Other Rituals

The following is the schedule of various daily pujas at Mahakaleshwar temple.

Schedule of Pujas

Bhasma Aarti*	4:00 to 6:00 a.m.
Naivedya Aarti	7:30 to 8:15 a.m.
Morning Puja	7:00 to 7:30 a.m.
Midday Puja	10:00 to 10:30 a.m.
Abhishek with water stops	5:00 p.m.
Evening Aarti	6:30 to 7:00 p.m.
Shyana Aarti	10:30 p.m.
Closing time	11:00 p.m.

Summer timings

Morning Aarti	7:00 to 7:45 a.m.
Evening Aarti	7:00 to 7:30 p.m.

* Lord Mahakaleshwar's is probably the only temple in the world where the Bhasma Aarti is performed routinely. This aarti is offered to Lord Mahakaleshwar every morning during 4:00 – 6:00 a.m. amidst vedic chants, recitation of stotras, and the sounds of cymbals, conchs, and *damaru*. The *bhasma* (ash) is prepared by burning dried cowdung. A representative of the Akhil Bhartiya Mahanirvani Akhada offers the *bhasma*. During Bhasma Aarti

no one enters the sanctum sanctorum for worship wearing common clothes. Only males wearing silk clothes are allowed to enter. The devotees witness the aarti from the *sabhagriha* just outside the *garbhagriha*.

Bhasma Aarti is performed in the afternoon of Phalgun Amavasya on the day after Mahashivaratri after removing Lord's sehra (bridegroom's floral crown). This happens only once a year.

The pujas and *anushthanas* undertaken in the Mahakaleshwar temple are: daily *Jalabhishek*, daily *Panchamrita* puja, *Abhishek* with *Rudra Ashtadhyayee, Laghu rudra, Maha rudra, Mahamrityunjaya Japa* and *Havan*.

Other Festivals and Programmes

Sl No.	Month	Paksha	Tithi	Event/Programme
1.	Chaitra	Shukla	Pratipada	Nav samvatsara (new year) puja of Mahakaleshwar and Chandramouleswar, panchang puja
2.	Vaisakh	Krishna	Pratipada	Continuous Jaldhara Abhishek for the next two months
3.	Vaisakh	Shukla	Akshaya tritiya	Gifting pitchers and fruits
4.	Jyestha	Krishna	Somavati Amavasya	Mahakaleshwar darshan
5.	Ashadh	Shukla	Guru Purnima	Beginning of special decorations for Shravana and Chaturmas
6.	Shravana	Krishna	Every Monday	Savari (procession)
7.	Shravana	Krishna	Amavasya	Deep puja
8.	Shravana	Shukla	Every Monday	Savari

9.	Shravana	Shukla	Nag Panchami	Nagchandreshwara and Panchanag Shringara of Mahakaleshwar
10.	Shravana	Shukla	Purnima	Raksha Sutra Parva, Bhog and special decoration
11.	Bhadrapada	Krishna	Every Monday	Savari (up to Amavasya)
12.	Bhadrapada	Krishna	Ashtami	Janmashtami after the evening aarti
13	Ashwin	Krishna	Ekadashi	Uma Sanji Mahotsava
14.	Ashwin	Shukla	Dvitiya	Uma Sanji Visarjan Savari
15.	Ashwin	Shukla	Dashmi	Vijaya Dashmi, Shami puja and Savari
16.	Ashwin	Shukla	Purnima	Sharadotsava, Dugdha Vitran
17	Kartik	Krishna	Chaturdashi	Abhyanga Snana and Annakoot
18.	Kartik	Krishna	Amavasya	Deepavali
19.	Kartik	Shukla	Every Monday	Savari
20.	Kartik	Shukla	Vaikunth Chaturdashi	Hari-Har-Milan Savari at midnight
21.	Margshirsha	Krishna	Every Monday	Savari
22.	Pausha	Shukla	Dhan Sankranti	Annakoot
23.	Magha	Krishna	Vasant Panchami	Special puja
24.	Phalgun	Krishna	Panchami	Different shringaras of Mahakaleshwar are done all nine days from Sashthi to Shivaratri
25.	Phalgun	Krishna	Trayodashi	Mahashivaratri Mahotsava, special puja
26.	Phalgun	Krishna	Amavasya	Sehra Darshan and noon Bhasma Aarti
27.	Phalgun	Shukla	Dvitiya	Panch-Svarup Shringara darshan, special puja
28.	Phalgun	Shukla	Purnima	Holika Utsava after evening aarti
29.	Chaitra	Krishna	Panchami	Ranga Panchami, Flag Mahotsava, Yajna, Puja and procession of Mahakala Dhwaja (flag) in the city

Apart from puja, *archana, abhishek, aarati* and such other rituals regularly performed in the Mahakaleshwar temple throughout the year, the following auspicious occasions/events deserve special mention.

Nitya Yatra

Conduct of a *yatra* (procession) is narrated in the Avanti Khanda of *Skanda Purana*. According to this, in this *yatra*, first the *yatri* (participant in the procession) takes bath in the holy Shipra. Afterwards he/she visits the temples of Nagachandreshwar, Koteshwar, Mahakaleshwar, goddess Avantika, goddess Harsiddhi, and Agastheswar.

Sravana Mahotsava (Festival)

On every Monday of the month of Sravana up to Amavasya in the dark fortnight of the Bhadrapada, and also from the bright fortnight of Kartika to the dark fortnight of Margashirsha, the savari (procession) of Lord Mahakaleshwar passes through the streets of Ujjain.

The last *savari* in Bhadrapada is celebrated with great pomp and show and is attended by lakhs of people.The procession of Mahakaleshwar on Vijayadasami festival visiting the celebrations at Dashahara maidan is also very attractive. As Mahakaleshwar is the Lord of dance and music, this time top ranking artists of India visit the temple to offer their homage to Lord Mahakaleshwar.

Harihara Milan

On Baikuntha Chaturdasi, Lord Mahakaleshwar visits this temple in a procession to meet Lord Dwarakadhisa (Hari) during

✷ *A panoramic view of Mahakala Temple in the night*

midnight. Later on, in a similar procession on that very night Dwarakadhisa visits Mahakaleshwar temple. This festival is the symbol of oneness between the two great Lords.

Narak Chaturdashi

On Narak Chaturdashi day Lord Mahakaleshwar is bathed with aromatic herbal pastes. This is called the Abhanga Snana. From this day onwards the deity is bathed with lukewarm water. After the Bhasma Aarti a special puja is offered.

platform. The idol is fitted onto one of the walls. Its open mouth serves as the channel to pour liquor which is an ingredient to worship in Bhairavi Chakras of the *tantriks*. It is said that the liquor poured into the mouth disappears even though apparently there is no drainage to carry it. It is likely that there is a subterranean channel. The temple is surrounded by high walls with a large stone *deepastambha* facing it. The *deepastambha* has 216 stone lamps which are lit on special occasions and important festivals such as Deepavali, Navaratri, and Shivaratri.

✴ *Deepastambha with 216 stone lamps*

Kalabhairava, being the deity of the leftist group of followers of the *tantriks*, has peculiar characteristics. The attendant animals as in the cases of Ganesha and Shiva, also are associated with the deity. Dogs are the pet animals as attendants of Kalabhairava, as the attendant animals of Shiva and Ganesha are Nandi (bull) and mouse, respectively.

Tantric rituals were usually performed in cremation grounds. This temple stands on the banks of the Shipra. The other bank of the river has a burning *ghat*. The cult of *tantra* is an unorthodox

✷ *Inside view of Kalabhairava temple*

secret cult with brawny black magic overtones. Although *tantra* practices on the sly are said to keep the enemy at bay, missing the target can spell doom to the practitioner.

Several *sadhus* or holy men with ash-smeared bodies and long matted hair can be spotted around the Kalabhairava temple which is an important centre of tantric worship.

Some people believe that this might have been a great temple during the Paramara period. Images of Shiva, Parvati, Vishnu, and Ganesha have been recovered from this place. The temple appears to have been rebuilt with the remains of the old temple. Beautiful paintings in the Malwa style once decorated the temple walls. Only traces of these are seen now. The temple to the right of the courtyard is dedicated to Vithala. To the left is a *dharamshala* (shelter for pilgrims and devotees). A Shivalinga is enshrined under a banyan tree inside the periphery of the temple opposite Nandi who is said to have carried Shiva to the battle against the demons. The village of Bhairagarh, famous for its textile printing takes its name from Kalabhairava temple and is located nearby.

Devotees visit the Kalabhairava temple throughout the year. The temple becomes very crowded especially during the festival of Mahashivaratri, when the ardent devotees flock in large numbers from various parts of the country, mostly from Gujarat and Maharashtra.

Patal Bhairavi cave lies on the north of the entrance to the temple. During the Mughal period, a monk named Jadarupa lived here. Mughal emperors Akbar and Jehangir came here when they visited Malwa.

A stone slab fitted on the plinth area to the left of the inner entrance to the temple records that renovation and extension of the temple complex was carried out at a cost of ₹ 12 lakh by His Holiness Jagadguru Sri Sri Sri Balagangadharanath Mahaswamiji, President, Sriadichunchanagiri Maha Sansthana Math, Karnataka, on 29 April 2004. There is no management committee for the maintenance of the temple. The maintenance is looked after by a few priests.

The temple complex is spread over a large area which includes the residences of the priests. The majestic gate built on a high level displays the brilliance of late mediaeval architecture. On either side of the entrance are parking areas for tourists' vehicles, and several small shops for meeting the needs of the devotees and tourists.

Chintaman Ganesha Temple

Chintaman Ganesha temple is located across the Shipra on the Fatehabad railway line. The temple is an antediluvian shrine dating back to 11th to 12th centuries CE. It is believed that the temple was built when the Paramaras ruled over Malwa. The temple was once renovated by Ahilyabhai Holkar of Indore. A water tank and a boundary wall were also built then. It is believed that on his way back to Ayodhya after killing Ravana, Lord Rama rested here. To quench their thirst, Lakshmana dug out water from earth with his arrow which has since become the water tank. That is why the tank is called Banganga.

This ancient temple is highly revered as one of the most visited shrines in Ujjain. Wholly made out in stone, the temple is dedicated to Lord Ganesha, who is regarded by Hindus as the lord of 'beginnings'. He is also known as 'Chintaharan', literally

Chintaman Ganesha Temple

✷ *Idol of Chintaman Ganesha*

meaning 'remover of worries'. The temple is thronged by crowds of people, especially on Wednesdays, in the month of Chaitra to worship Lord Ganesha. People also come here in large numbers on Saturdays as well as on other days, too. A large number of couples come here to seek the blessings of the great God before or after their marriage.

The idol is believed to be *swayambhu* (self-manifested). Riddhi and Siddhi, the consorts of Lord Ganesha, are seated on either side of the Lord. The finely-carved stone pillars in the assembly hall belong to the Paramara period (9th to 12th century CE). The white shrine defines the sanctity of the temple. The temple also has the idol of Lord Vishnu in its vicinity. Lords Ganesha and Vishnu are worshipped here with great devotion.

The very appearance of the temple reveals its primitive characteristics. Till date the temple has kept its age-old charm and sanctity. The trust of the devotees in this temple makes it all the more sanctified.

Harsiddhi Temple

Harsiddhi temple occupies a special place in the many ancient sacred places in Ujjain. The image of goddess Harsiddhi, painted in vermilion, is situated between the images of Mahalakshmi and Mahasaraswati. Harsiddhi Mata is probably none other than Annapurna. The goddess was the tutelary deity of the Paramara rulers. According to a legend from *Shiva Purana*, Lord Shiva was greatly disturbed after the death of his consort, Sati. Overwhelmed by grief, Shiva, also called the Destroyer of the Universe, decided not to part with her body. He carried it wherever

✷ *Harisiddhi Temple*

he went. Greatly distressed by this situation, the rest of the divine community cut her body into several pieces and threw in Mrityulok, the land of mortals. The places where the parts of Sati's body fell became *Shaktipeeths*, or centres of the female manifest form of cosmic energy. Sati's elbow fell in Ujjain where the Harsiddhi temple was located. It, therefore, became a Shaktipeeth in the tantric tradition. There is also an interesting story in the *Skanda Purana* about the manner in which goddess Chandi acquired the epithet of Harsiddhi.

Once when Lord Shiva and Parvati were in mount Kailash, two demons, Chand and Prachand, tried to force their way in. On Shiva's command, Chandi destroyed them. Pleased, Shiva bestowed upon her the epithet of one who vanquishes all. According to a local folk tradition, King Chandragupta Vikramaditya worshipped Harsiddhi.

✷ *Idol of Harsiddhi in the temple*

In the centre of the temple is a rock smeared with turmeric paste and vermilion. This is believed to represent the head of emperor Chandragupta Vikramaditya (circa

380–415 CE) offered to Goddess Durga, the symbol of power, on the eve of the festival of Dussehra. Shakti, the female principle of primaeval cosmic energy, is propitiated with sacrifices. It is also believed that emporer Vikramaditya brought Harsiddhi from Miyam Village near Muldharaka, 25 km away from Somnath, where there is a temple of Harshad Devi. Harshad Devi and Harsiddhi are the same. It is believed that Harsiddhi sits in Ujjain during daytime and in Miyam village during the night. In both places similar kind of thrones are arranged.

The temple has two unique pine-shaped iron lampstands. They have 726 lamps on them and they are 15 feet high. It is marvellous to see the lit lampstands. Hundreds of burning lamps make a wondrous sight. They are always lit during Navaratri, the nine-day festival celebrated in October, and dedicated to Goddess Durga. The red temple, another ancient Hindu structure beyond the lampstands symbolising the potency of Durga, is characteristic of Maratha art.

Another feature of the temple is the presence of Sri Yantra (symbol of Shakti), or nine triangles that represent nine names of Durga. A *yantra* is symbolic of the cosmos and is used while meditating. Each division of a Yantra is symbolic of Shakti, the power of the cosmic energy that has to be propitiated with sacrifices. Also enshrined in this temple is the famous dark vermilion-stained image of Annapurna, the Goddess of Nourishment. The inner roof of the temple is covered with exquisitely beautiful multi-coloured paintings showing various mythological stories related to the Goddess and other divinities.

✷ *Pine-shaped twin iron lampstands with 726 lamps*

✷ *Inner roof of Harsiddhi temple*

There are a few more temples in the premises such as Chintaharan Ganesha temple and Karkoteshwar Mahadeva temple. Karkoteshwar Mahadeva temple, one of the main temples out of the 84 Mahadeva temples, stands just opposite to the main temple. Special worships and celebrations are offered here in the months of Chaitra and Ashwin. It is also believed that goddess Harsiddhi remains at Koila Dungar temple in Porbander for twelve hours every day and comes to Ujjain in the evening during aarti time. There is also an ancient well in the temple premises. An artistic pillar adorns the top of it.

Behind the Harsiddhi temple complex are the temples of Agastheswar, Sangameshwar, Dundeshwar, Damarukeshar, and Swarnajaleshwar, all belonging to the group of 84 Mahadeva temples. A temple of Santoshi Mata is also located there. Kapalmatrika ka sthan, a sacred spot, is very near to the temple complex. At the western side behind the temple can be seen a large idol of Hanuman in sitting posture. The temple also has a pool known as Mahesh Kund in the south-east corner.

Situated on an elevated area on the western bank of Rudrasagar, the temple has four entrances and attracts thousands of devotees and tourists throughout the year, especially during Navaratri. The maintenance and day-to-day affairs of the temple are looked after by a management committee. The temple has the collection of a few beautiful stone pillars on which are carved figures of various gods and goddesses. These stone pillars, dated the late medieval period, may have been collected from the nearby areas to add more antique look to the temple complex.

Gadkalika Temple

Gadkalika temple is situated in suburban Ujjain, about two miles from the town. It is dedicated to goddess Kalika ('the black' fearsome goddess of death and destruction, also known as Chamunda). Truth is epitomised in Goddess Kalika. She is the premordial energy of the cosmos, and is worshipped as Shakti—the sustaining principle of life. She incarnates the

consummate beauty of death. She incarnates the perfect beauty of life, simultaneously violent and tender, grotesque and beatific. Shiva, her consort, personifies Shivam—all that is good on earth. He is the benefactor of all. Shiva and Kali together become the quintessence of the concept 'Satyam Shivam Sundaram'.

Legend has it that Kalidasa, the greatest Sanskrit poet and dramatist and the chief of the nine gems (*nava ratna*) in the court of emporer Vikramaditya, acquired his legendary literary skills due to his devotion to goddess Gadkalika. Images and bricks, and part of the plinth belonging to the Sunga (1st century BCE), Gupta (4th century CE) and Paramara (10th century CE) periods were recovered from the basement of the temple. Emperor Harshavardhan got this temple renovated in the 7th century CE. It

✷ *Garbhagriha of Gadkalika temple*

Previous page: *Gadkalika temple*

✴ *Goddess Kalika, the goddess of death and destruction*

✴ *Deepasthambha with 108 lamps*

was again renovated during the Paramara period (10th century CE). It is also reported that in 1944 CE, the then priest Shri Siddhanath Maharaja got this temple renovated. The temple has been rebuilt in modern times by the erstwhile Gwalior state. A beautiful sculpture of Yakshini belonging to the 4th–5th century CE was recovered from this place. It has been preserved at Bharti Kala Bhawan Museum, Ujjain.

The Gadkalika temple is an important place for tantric worship. The temple also has idols of Mahalakshmi on the one side and Saraswati on the other. An old statue of Lord Ganesha is placed behind the temple.

As has been reported, the archaeologists excavated this area in 1946. Based on the recovered ruins and other archaeological findings they have concluded that this place was part of the kingdom of Chandra Pradyota during the time of Gautam Buddha. His daughter Vasavadatta fell in love with Udayan, the king of Kausambi. This story is also narrated in *Kathasaritsagar*, Bhasa's *Vasavadatta* and Kalidasa's *Meghadutam*.

As the temple is located on a hillock, its picturesque natural surroundings add extra elegance to the complex. A number of devotees and tourists visit the temple every day, specially on Fridays when special pujas are performed to appease the goddess.

The utensils used for offering pujas are of different types and shapes. These days, however, stainless steel utensils are also used, not only those made of brass and copper. The priests belong to the Nath pujari community, which has the expertise to perform tantric worship.

The temple is looked after and maintained by a family of Nath priests, who reside in the temple complex itself.

There are two stone *deepasthambhas* with 108 lamps each on either side of the entrance to the temple. These *deepasthambhas* are lightened on specific occasions such as Deepavali.

Mangalnath Temple

Mangalnath Temple

Dedicated to Lord Shiva, Mangalnath temple is greatly revered in Ujjain. According to *Matsya Purana*, Mangalnath is said to be the birthplace of Mars (Mangal). The temple looks down upon a vast expanse of the Shipra waters and fills the onlooker with an indescribable sense of peace. A marvellous shrine located far away from the flurry of the city life, it offers unimaginable sense of tranquility to visitors. The temple is situated on a hillock. It is said

manner. This is the only temple in the country where special pujas are performed for those who have Mangal *dosh*. A large puja hall has been constructed for the exclusive use of devotees to offer pujas. Priests of the temple perform these pujas on demand from devotees who come from different parts of the country specially on Tuesdays and Sundays.

The temple is administered by a managing committee which is responsible for its maintenance, renovation, and related activities.

Bade Ganeshji Temple

Bade Ganeshji Temple

Bade Ganeshji temple is located near the tank of the Mahakaleshwar temple. Ganesha, the son of Shiva and Parvati, is believed to be the most benevolent God. The temple is famous for the grand idol of Ganesha with Riddhi and Siddhi with folded hands on either side. It is considered to be one of the largest statues of Lord Ganesha in India. At the feet of Ganesha a mouse, his vehicle, is shown holding a laddu. There is also

Idol of Lord Ganesha in Bade Ganeshji temple

✷ *Shivalinga, Ganesha idol, and other idols inside Bade Ganeshji temple*

a *panchamukhi* (five-faced) image of Hanuman, made of eight metals (*ashtadhatu*), in the middle of the temple. People visit the temple to obtain blessings of both Ganesha and Hanuman.

The temple is not very old. It was built by Pandit Suryanarayan Vyas. There are some mini temples inside the temple complex, as well as idols of other divinities such as the Navagrahas and idols of Shiva and Durga which also attract the attention of devotees. As the temple is located very near to the Mahakaleshwar temple

✷ *Panchmukhi image of Lord Hanuman made of eight metals*

complex, people visiting that temple usually visit this temple also, specially on Sundays, Mondays, Tuesdays, and Wednesdays.

Gopal Temple

The huge Gopal temple is dedicated to Gopal Krishna. It was constructed by Maharani Baija Bai, the able queen of Maharaja Daulat Rao Scindia in 1833 CE. It is a fine specimen of Maratha architecture. Besides that of Gopal Krishna, the images of Shiva, Parvati, Garuda, and Baija Bai are also installed in the

Gopal Temple

✷ *Garbhagriha of Gopal Temple*

sanctum of the temple. The temple is surrounded by a high wall, and has a lofty and ornate gateway with distinctive *bangaldar* roof. The *garbhagriha* is inlaid with marble, and the doors of the temple are silver plated. Lord Krishna's two feet tall statue is moulded in silver and is placed on a marble inlaid altar.

It is well-known that the silver-plated doors of the inner sanctum of the famous Somnath temple in Gujarat were taken by Mahmud of Ghazni to Ghazni in Afghanistan in 1026 CE. The Afghan invader Mahmud Shah Abdali later took those to Lahore from where Maharaja Scindia recovered them. The Maharaja later installed them in the Gopal temple.

✷ *The main entrance of Gopal temple*

✷ *A mosque stands next to Gopal temple*

Gopal temple is located in the middle of the market area, right in the heart of the city of Ujjain. The temple, therefore, always remains crowded with visitors and devotees.

The most important festivals celebrated in the temple are Janmashtami in the month of Bhadra (August–September) and Holi in February–March. Another important festival on the 14th day of the bright fortnight of Kartik is Hari–Har Milan. In the night Mahakaleshwar takes a *savari* and visits the Gopal temple where he offers *Bilva patra* to Dwarkadhish. In a retrun *savari* the same night Dwarkadhish offers a tulsi garland to Lord Mahakaleshwar. A *parva* unifying the Shaiva and Vaishnava sects is celebrated at the Mahakaleshwar temple.

Triveni Navagraha Temple

Triveni Navagraha temple is dedicated to the nine planets of the solar system. Situated on the Triveni ghat of Shipra, the temple attracts large crowds on Amavasya falling on Saturdays. The temple was in the past known as Shani mandir.

✷ *A small temple under an old tree in the Navagraha temple complex*

Facing page:
Above: *Painted idols of Navagraha*
Below: *Shops in front of Navagraha temple*

Page 81: *Triveni Navagraha temple*

In India, astronomy and astrology share an ancient bond. A legend which recalls the birth of Moon and Mars in Ujjain indicates that they were studied here even in ancient times. According to astrological beliefs, each planet exercises an influence on the lives of people living on this planet. Furthermore, if their influence is negative on our lives they need to be propitiated. Worshippers offer flowers, coconuts, and vermilion, as also mustard oil to the idol of Mangal, which is considered to exercise the most negative influence. Hindu geographers marked the first meridian at Ujjain, adding a greater significance to the temple.

Triveni Navagraha temple is located on the road to Indore at the confluence of Shipra and two other rivulets. The temple is about 150 years old. This temple has become more popular recently. There is, however, hardly any reference to this temple in the ancient texts.

Sandipani Ashram

Inner view of Sandipani Ashram

Sandipani Ashram is located near Mangalnath temple on the bank of river Shipra. Ujjain, apart from its political and religious importance, enjoyed the reputation of being a great seat of learning as early as the Mahabharata period. According to puranic traditions Lord Krishna, Balaram and their friend Sudama, received regular instructions in the Ashram of *kulaguru* Sandipani.

✷ *Gomti Kund*

Ankapata, near the Ashram, is believed to be the place used by Lord Krishna for washing his writing tablets. The numerals 1–100 on a stone are believed to have been engraved by Guru Sandipani.

A sacred tank known as Gomti Kund exists within the precincts of the Ashram, where Krishna is believed to have merged the waters of all the holy rivers so that his Guru would not have to travel to distant places on pilgrimage. The kund has been referred to in the puranas as a source of water supply to the Ashram in the olden days. An image of the seated Nandi belonging to the Sunga-Kushana period can be found near the kund.

There is a Shiva temple in the Sandipani Ashram. Here a *nag* (snake) is shown crawling by the side of the lingam. It may be mentioned here that in most of the Shiva temples in the country *nag* is invariably found wound around the lingam.

✷ *Miniature stone temples in the Sandipani Ashram complex*

Above: *An idol of Nandi belonging to the Sunga-Kushana period*

✷ *Shiva Temple in Sandipani Ashram complex*

The followers of the Vallabha sect regard this place as the 73rd of the 84 seats of Vallabhacharya who delivered discourses throughout India in the beginning of the 16th century CE. Vallabhacharya meditated here under a banyan tree which is believed to be 500 years old.

The Sandipani Ashram gets several visitors from different parts of the country, especially from Gujarat and Maharashtra. They visit this place after paying tributes at the Mangalnath temple which is located nearby.

Other Monuments

Ram Janardan temple, Nagarkot ki Rani temple and Choubis Khamba gate, located near the Mahakaleshwar temple complex, are important monuments.

Ram Janardan Temple

Ram Janardan temple, built by Mirza Raja Jai Singh in the 17th century CE is situated on the western bank of Vishnu Sagar located on the west of Gomti kund in the Sandipani ashram complex. It is a combination of two temples, in which Rama, Sita, Lakshmana, and Janardana Vishnu are worshipped. The structural art of both the temples is very attractive. The boundary wall and the tank were constructed later during the Maratha period in the 18th century CE.

Beautiful specimens of Maratha paintings can be seen on the walls of both the temples. Besides attractive scenes from the lives of Rama (*kumbha*) of nectar lying at the bed of the ocean of milk (*Kshirsagar*). Drinking nectar could make one immortal. To recover the nectar, they needed to churn the ocean. They used the fabled Mandara mountain as a churning rod and the great serpent Vasuki as the churning rope. Both gods and demons together churned the ocean for a long time. They found the seven precious jewels including a golden *kumbha* (pitcher) containing *amrita* (nectar). It had earlier been agreed upon by the two sides that whatever emerged from churning of the ocean of milk would be shared equally between them.

However, when the pitcher of nectar emerged, the gods got scared and thought that if the demons were allowed to have their share, they would become immortal and could never be destroyed. To save this situation, Indra, the king of gods, asked his son Jayant to flee with the *amrita kumbha* (pitcher of nectar). When the demons realised what was happening, a hot pursuit ensued. The demons chased Jayant all over the world. During the chase, drops of nectar

✷ *Kumbha Mela at Ujjain*

fell at four sites, namely Haridwar and Prayag on the Ganga, Ujjain on the Shipra, and Nasik on the Godavari. It is believed that the chase continued for 12 days and nights. This is why *Kumbha Mela* (pitcher festival) is celebrated at Ujjain every twelve years.

This legend is so deeprooted in the minds of the people that it is considered to be a historical fact on the basic characteristics of the temple culture of Ujjain.

Harsiddhi Temple

There is an interesting legend in the *Skanda Purana* about how goddess Chandi acquired the epithet of Harsiddhi. Once when Shiva and Parvati were alone in Mount Kailash, two demons, Chand and Prachand, tried to force their way in. As commanded by Shiva, Chandi destroyed them. Pleased at this Shiva bestowed upon Chandi the epithet of Harsiddhi (one who vanquishes all). This legend is still considered by the people as an authentic evidence

✷ *Savari of Mahakaleshwar reaches River Shipra*

of Goddess Harsiddhi's acquiring the deserving epithet from Shiva. Even the Harsiddhi temple is believed to be a Shaktipeeth as the elbow of Sati fell at where the temple is located.

Banganga Water Tank in Chintaman Ganesha Temple

✷ *Lakshman Babri, also known as Banganga*

There is also a legend about a Banganga Water Tank in Chintaman Ganesha temple. It is said that while returning to Ayodhya after killing Ravana, Rama and the entire group rested here. To quench their thirst, Lakshmana dug out water using his arrow. This is why the water tank is called Banganga (arrow Ganga).

Mahashivaratri

The legend on the Mahashivaratri festival is very interesting. Shivaratri (the great night of Shiva) is celebrated on the 13th day of Phalgun dark fortnight. On this day devotees observe fast.

Once a hunter set out to hunt. He came near a pond and climed a *bel* tree (sacred tree to Shiva). Sitting on the tree he waited for animals. But since the leaves obstructed his vision, he plucked and threw down a few leaves. These leaves fell on a Shivalinga under the tree. When a herd of deer came to drink water, the hunter took aim at a female deer. She cried out to the hunter, 'Please wait for a moment. Before you shoot, let me go home and meet my young ones for the last time. Afterwards you may take my life at your pleasure'.

The hunter permitted the female deer to go home. He continued to sit on the tree waiting for her return. Having to wait for the whole night, the hunter undertook a forced fast. He had inadvertently thrown the sacred *bel* leaves on the Shivalinga. He had also uttered the name of Shiva. Thus, without knowing what he was doing, he had observed the Mahashivaratri vow. Unknown to him, his heart was filled with sentiments of mercy, kindness, and love. Before dawn the mother deer came back with the entire herd. 'Now you may take my life at your pleasure', she said.

Seeing the female deer's honesty the hunter's heart further softened. He did not want to kill her. Lord Shiva was so pleased with them that he took them to heaven. Both the female deer and the hunter can be seen at night in the sky among the stars in the constellation of Orion (*Mrugshirsh* star).

Shivalingam in Mahakaleshwar Temple

A powerful demon, who lived on Ratnamal mountain, attacked Avanti (now Ujjain) and killed a Brahmin sage by setting him afire. The angry Lord Shiva opened his third eye and burnt the demon to ashes. A *Shivalingam* appeared on the spot where Lord Shiva opened his third eye and killed the demon. Mahakaleshwar temple was built on the spot.

Myths and Life in Ujjain

It thus appears that these myths and legends constantly remind the people of their intimate relationship with their favourite gods and goddesses. These legends and myths are so deep-rooted in the minds of the people that they are utterly convinced about their authenticity.

The relationship between life and myth in Ujjain and nearby areas is like the seed-and-tree relationship; each gives rise to the other. Myths are passed on from generation to generation. Children grow up with certain cultural preoccupations that lead them to repeat myths. Basically, the cultural patterns prevalent in Ujjain and its suburbs are based on the concepts of cultural tradition, having a unity of its own, and which is reflected through fairs and festivals, cultural performances, oral literatures, mythologies, beliefs, practices, and customs.

A close study of the data collected reflects a pattern of temple culture the manifestations of which relates to people's observance of day-to-day rituals, their active participation in the temple fairs and festivals, and their faith in the gods' benevolence. Even today the people of Ujjain and its adjoining areas firmly believe that a *puja* performed with unstinted faith at any of the temples in Ujjain can bring peace and happiness, and fulfill their cherished desires.

The temple cultural geography of the holy city of Ujjain reveals a unifying vision that reaches out to the cardinal directions to establish the sacred ground of pilgrimage. The sites of fairs and festivals, especially on the sacred banks of holy river Shipra, and in the temples dedicated to various gods and goddesses, should be looked upon with utmost reverence as the eternal sources of religious and socio-cultural revelation. There also co-exists an age-old folk tradition of arranging cultural performances on various festive occasions. This landscape of cultural exposition ensures, within a traditional framework, a process of learning, absorbing, and creating that establishes the cultural unity of this part of the Malwa region of Madhya Pradesh.

Fairs and Festivals

Fairs and festivals not only play an important role in the socio-cultural life of the people of Ujjain, but also are an integral part of its temple culture. During these occasions, music and cultural performances in honour of the gods or goddess are arranged. The festival also involves different kinds of rituals. The *mela* (fair) is also a religious festival as it is set by the motions and positions of stars, moon, and the planets.

Certain festivals, namely Baisakhi, Basant Panchami and Makarsankranti, are celebrated according to lunar day (*tithi*) or as set by the motions and positions of the stars, moon, and the planets. Basant Panchami (also known as Sripanchami) is celebrated on the 5th day of the bright half (*shuklapaksha*) in the month of Magha (January–February), while Baisakhi is celebrated on the full moon day of the month of Baisakha (April–May). Makarsankranti is circumstances the Mela is not celebrated. It is said that bathing in the Shipra on such an occasion confers the bather the merit of having taken nectar. *Moksha*, or eternal redemption, is the ultimate desire of every religious-minded Hindu and he can attain it here in a trice. The Kumbha Mela held at Ujjain is known as Simhastha because of Jupiter's (Vrihaspati's) presence in the house of Leo (Simha).

Lakhs of Hindus bathe in the Shipra during the month-long Simhastha fair from Chaitra Purnima to Baisakhi Purnima. Saints, mentors of various orders of Hindu faith, Sankaracharyas and ascetics reach here from various parts of the country. Udasi Nagas, Nagas, and Dashnami Sadhus, Vaishnavites, Shaivites, Kabirpanthis and followers of Ramanujacharya, Chaitanyaswami, Madhavacharya, Vallabhacharya and others converse here during Simhastha and set their camps. Pilgrims have the opportunity to benefit from their wisdom and company. Inspiring and scholarly discourses by seers, round-the-clock hymn singing and discussions continue during the month-long fair. Pilgrims in thousands participate in these activities to enlighten themselves. It is also an occasion for initiation into various religious cults.

Ten important spots related to Kumbha Mela

Sl No.	Name	Important for
1	Datta akhada	Naga sadhus
2	Nrisimha ghat	Paramahams sadhus
3	Gadkalika temple	Nathpanthi sadhus
4	Gomati Kund	Pushtimarg sadhus of Vallabh sampraday
5	Ankapad	Vairagi sadhus

6	Mangalnath temple	Tyagi akhada sadhus
7	Ranika Bagh	Dadu Panthi sadhus, Kabir Panthi sadhus and Ram Snehi Panthi sadhus
8	Hanumanth Bagh	Udasi Sant sadhus
9	Mullamadari ka Bagh	Nanak Panthi sadhus
10	Mullapura	Swami Narayan sadhus and Prajapita Brahmakumari sadhus

During Kumbha Mela Ujjain caters to hundreds of thousands of pilgrims and *sadhus* (saints). Majestically slow and soothingly decorated elephants tread the fair ground adding extra flavour to the city. A visit to Ujjain during Kumbha Mela is really an experience of divinity.

Mahashivaratri is the most important festival in Ujjain after Kumbha Mela. This is because Shiva is the most worshipped God in Ujjain. The tradition of celebrating Mahashivaratri is so deep rooted in the minds of the people that the festival is performed not only with great fervour and austerity, but also as a cult practice which may have its origin in 'prehistoric tribalism'.

Mahashivaratri is celebrated with great fervor in Ujjain, especially in Mahakaleshwar temple. Maharshi Narad advised mankind to fast on this day and pray to the all powerful Shiva so that in all his kindness he pardons our sins committed in the past three lives.

On the day of the festival devotees observe fast the whole day and keep vigil throughout the night. Devotees then bathe in water boiled with black sesame seeds to wash away bodily impurities. They then put on new clothes. They wash the Lingam with milk and perform religious rites. They put haldi and kumkum on the Lingam and decorate it with a garland of white and pink lotus flowers. The Lingam is worshipped with *bel* leaves. *Aarti* is performed and *bhajans* are sung to invoke his blessings. The aroma of lighted agarbattis seems to float in the air. The chinning of the bells as well as melodious devotional songs reverberate from temples.

Vasant Panchami is celebrated in Magha (January–February) as one of the early festivals of the year. The festival is celebrated to welcome spring and to bid goodbye to winter. On this day people wear yellow dresses and decorate idols with yellow clothes. Saraswati Puja is also performed in the city with lot of enthusiasm.

Holi is the festival of colour, falling during February–March. New dresses are bought for the festival, especially for married daughters and their children.

Holi falls on 'Dwadashi', i.e. on the 12th day of the waxing moon of Phalgun. 'Rang Pashi' takes place three days earlier to Holi, when all the family members get together in the evening. Holi is celebrated not only in houses, but also in institutions, colleges, and other places. Rang Panchami is celebrated five days after Holi.

Even today Holi continues to be celebrated, with its initial role of appreciating nature, drawing inspiration and spirit from nature. Holi is the favourite of believers and sceptics both. Its reach spreads across caste, class, and gender. Holi exalts the significance of the bond between siblings, and that between humans and other life forms.

Ram Navami falls in April. It reminds us of the birth of Sri Ram, the 7th incarnation of Lord Vishnu. On this day *pujas* are performed in the morning. As Sri Ram was born in the afternoon, elaborate *pujas* are performed in the afternoon. Some people observe fast on this day while some others take food only once.

Raksha Bandhan (*Rakhi*) is celebrated during July–August. This festival binds brothers and sisters in a close bond. On this day, the sister ties a *rakhi* on the right wrist of her brother. In return the brother gives gifts or money to his sister as a symbol of strengthening the love between them. The brother promises to protect his sister. Special *pujas* are also performed at home on this day by the daughters or the aunts.

Janmashtami (the birthday of Lord Krishna) falls in the month of Bhadra (July–August) eight days after *Raksha Bandhan*. The festival is celebrated in temples as well as homes. People observe either full or partial fast on this day. Special *pujas* or prayers are offered.

Dussehra is celebrated during September–October. Dussehra recalls the victory of Sri Ram over Ravana. On this day people make effigies of Ravana, his brother Kumbhakarna, and his son Meghnad. These effigies are filled with crackers and fireworks. At sunset, a person who makes up like Ram shoots an arrow into the navel of Ravana, which is said to be the container of a pot of nectar, the source of Ravana's power and invincibility.

According to an epic legend, Ram was a great devotee of Goddess Durga. Before killing Ravana he meditated before Durga for nine days. On the tenth day he killed Ravana, Kumbhakarna, and Meghnad. This day is considered to be very auspicious and important for the progress and prosperity of mankind.

Deepavali (*Diwali*) is considered the largest and grandest celebration in India. It is the festival of lights. The festival signifies the victory of good over evil. The killing of Ravana is also remembered on this day. It is the day Rama returned to Ayodhya after 14 years of exile. Commemorating the return of Rama, Sita, and Lakshmana, people celebrate *Deepavali* with bursting of crackers, and by lighting up their houses with lamps.

The 13th day of the dark fortnight, that is two days before Deepavali, is known as Dhanteras. On this day people purchase new utensils and clean, wash, and paint their homes.

The day prior to Deepavali is known as *Chhoti* Deepavali. On this day Hanuman, the greatest devotee of Lord Ram, arrived in Ayodhya to give information about the arrival of Ram, Lakhsman, and Sita the next day.

On the day of Deepavali, morning bath in a holy river is considered very auspicious. Special *pujas* followed by *rangoli* and *mehendi* increase the beauty of the festival.

Navaratri comes twice in a year. One is in the month of Chaitra (March–April) (Vasantheya Navaratri) and the other in the month of Ashvin (September–October) (Saradiya Navaratri). Devi Bhagavati is adorned and worshipped during the Navaratri festivals.

✷ *The* Savari *(procession) of King Mahakaleshwar reaches river Shipra*

Savari (procession) of King Mahakaleshwar is another important festival that is celebrated with pomp and show. Lord Mahakaleshwar moves in the city in a palanquin to meet his subjects. Devotees from every nook and corner of the country gather here to have a glimpse of their beloved king.

The *savari* of Lord Mahakaleshwar is organised on every Monday in the month of Sravana. The event takes place in the evening between 4 p.m. and 7.30 p.m. Similar *savaris* take place on all Mondays of the month of Kartika as well as during Vijayadashami.

had a flat roof without a Shikhara. This style was perhaps taken to be the unique model of temple architecture of the classical period of Indian history.

Some data exist on the social and cultural status of the city. The political and economic factors made the city so important in the past due to its strategic location on the main artery of trade between North, South, and West. This in turn contributed to Ujjain acquiring a cultural splendour on its own which was equalled by very few other cities in India.

From the time of Chandra Pradyota Mahasena (Circa 6th century BCE) the people of Ujjain may have faced a number of challenges in the political as well as socio-cultural fronts with the spread of Buddhism and Jainism. But religious tolerance practised by the socio-cultural and religious groups paved the way for strengthening and promoting the city's tradition. In *Meghadutam* Kalidasa gives a lyrical description of Ujjain and its people which conjures up 'a vivid picture of a civilised attractive society, a leisured class, intensely practical and yet imbued with deeply religious and philosophical preoccupations'. During the 7th century CE Ujjain became a part of Harsha's empire. The city then was known as a centre of learning, of astronomical and mathematical research, and a home to the cultural heritage of Hinduism, Buddhism, and Jainism. The people then must have served the multiple purpose of catering to various interests in the political, social, cultural, and economic fields.

Later on also Ujjain remained under the political sway of the Pratiharas, the Rashtrakutas and the Paramaras. But the social, cultural, and economic growth of the city was not halted.

The civil society of Ujjain had to face a troubled period when the last Paramara ruler, Siladitya, was defeated by the Sultans of Mandu. The glory of Ujjain was lost in a morass of repeated attacks. Delhi Sultan Iltutmish systematically disecrated and destroyed temples. He destroyed not only Mahakaleshwar temple but also other religious and cultural centres. The nature of destruction clearly indicates that the invaders purposely wanted to destroy every major symbol of Hindu cultural heritage.

During early 17th century CE Ujjain was ruled by the Marathas. They resuscitated its decaying temple culture. Mahakaleshwar and Harsiddhi temples were reconstructed during this period. Ujjain finally passed on to the Scindias in 1750 CE. The Scindias also contributed a lot to the sustained development of modern Ujjain's temple culture which still plays an important role in the social and cultural lives of the people.

Since ancient times Ujjain has been visited by people from different regions and religions. Ujjain is widely known as the land of Gods. Pilgrims from all over India, especially from the neighbouring states, visit the city frequently. The influx of pilgrims thus opens a suitable channel of communication among different groups and with the local people of Ujjain. This interaction helps in building up a society devoid of social evils. Pilgrimage thus promotes inter-cultural communication as well as fundamental affinity of people, irrespective of race, caste, community, class, colour, and creed. It is true that Ujjain has the characteristics of a cosmopolitan city. However, the temples have an inseparable role on the social and cultural life of the people. No ceremony is complete without visiting the temple and praying to the deity. Even when a person falls sick or when major problems crop up, he prays at a temple.

In Ujjain the followers of different faiths, religions, and sects have lived together peacefully. The temple culture has been developed without any interference from any religious doctrine or practice, except during Muslim invasions. To this day the people uphold the age-old tradition of homogenous cultural identity. Our survey has revealed that entry into the temples is not restricted to any class or caste of devotees. They, however, need to be clean while entering the temple. They should also not take forbidden food or drinks before entering the temple premises. It may be noted that animal sacrifice was not in vogue in any of the temples in Ujjain including those dedicated to tantric worship.

The annual fairs and festivals held in temples also play a significant role in the life of the people. These festivals provide an opportunity for the urban and rural people to meet and interact, thus promoting unity among different communities. A fair or festival brings together different strata of society and develops a bond of friendship among them.

Ujjain's temple culture may be attributed to various factors such as religious beliefs and practices as well as patronisation of a number of devotees, religious leaders, and Royal dynastyies. It has also remained interactive and indissoluble with age-old tradition.

Role of River Shipra

River Shipra played an important role in the evolution and development of the temple culture of Ujjain. The river starts flowing from the Vindhyan range north of Dhar and falls into the Chambal river near Kalakheri village in Mandsaur district of Madhya Pradesh. It is written in Avanti Khanda of *Skanda Purana* that river Shipra would emancipate us from our sins and purify the soul if one stands a few moments praying on its bank. There are hundreds of Hindu shrines along the banks of the river and lakhs of Hindus bathe in this river during important festivals. *Skanda Purana* gives five names for Shipra, that is Jvarghani (destroyer of fever), Papaghani (destroyer of sins), Amrita sambhava (generator of nectar), Celestial Shipra (also known as Kshipra), and Vishnudehodbhava (born out of the body of Lord Vishnu). River Shipra is also referred to as Uttarvahini (that which flows to the north). There are several legends about river Shipra.

According to a *Skanda Purana* story, once Lord Shiva went to Vishnu with Kapala in his hand. He asked *bhiksha* (holy offerings of food) from Vishnu. Vishnu, instead of giving *bhiksha*, showed his index finger. Shiva became very angry. He threw his *trishula* (trident) at the finger. The blood from the injured finger filled

A panoramic view of river Shipra

the Kapala. The overflown blood fell on earth and became river Shipra. Some others believe that it is the blood of Lord Shiva that flows through Shipra.

As per another legend Shiva drank Halahala poison during amrita manthan to save the world. He stuck it in his throat. Later he decided to return it to the ocean. Shiva enquired of the rivers as to who was willing to carry Halahala to the ocean. None of the rivers, except Shipra, came forward. Shipra accepted the challenge because of her devotion to Lord Shiva. She accepted Halahala and carried it to the ocean very fast. That is how the river got its name Shipra (or Kshipra), or 'fast'.

According to *Kalika Purana* the legend of the origin of river Shipra goes like this: Meghatithi was conducting the wedding ceremony of her daughter Arundhati. Maharshi Vashishtha came there. He fell in the water which had been collected from celestial Shipra. The water which overflowed started to flow and it became the holy river Shipra.

Another legend from *Skanda Puarana* says that Daman, a sinner of Kikat, was travelling through the Mahakala forest. He felt very tired and slept under a tree. A snake bit him and he died in sleep. Lord Yama took away Daman's soul. A crow took a piece of the body in its beaks and flew away. But that piece of flesh fell in river Shipra. Because of that Daman was relieved of all his sins and became like Shiva. So Shipra is known as 'Papanashini' – destroyer of all sins.

Another legend in *Skanda Purana* records that Krishna fought with Vanasur who ran away and took refuge at the feet of Shiva. In order to save Vanasur, Shiva fought with Krishna. Shiva produced Birabhadra from his hairs and sent him in the form of a fever to Krishna's army. Krishna too sent a fever on the army of Shiva. Both armies took refuge in river Shipra and were immediately cured. Therefore Shipra is known as Jvarghani.

Another *Skanda Purana* legend says that once Shiva went begging to Nagaloka (the world of serpants). But he did not get anything. So he drank 21 *amrita kumbhas* (pots of nectar) by his third eye. Nagar complained to Vishnu who advised him to worship Mahakaleshwar. Lord Shiva told Nagar to fill the pots with water from river Shipra. Nagar did as commanded and found that the pots were again filled with nectar. Therefore Shipra came to be known as Amrita sambhava. According to yet another legend Shipra is the blood of Lord Vishnu who took the form of Narasimha to kill Hiranyakashipu, the demon. Therefore Shipra is also known as Vishnu Dehodbhava.

It is believed that taking bath in Shipra during Kumbha mela confers the merit of having taken nectar. The river is held in equal esteem as Ganga. Even the chanting of 'Shipra, Shipra' confers merit on a devotee. It is believed that a bath in Shipra on certain auspicious occasions, namely Ganga Dussehra, Kartik Purnima, Vaisakhi Purnima, and solar and lunar eclipses are of great religious significance.

River Shipra, Mahakaleshwar, Rudrasagar, Mansarovar, Baidyanath, River Saraswati, and Gaya are holy for *shraddha* (last rites) for departed souls of forefathers. Its water is so clean that it is popularly known as Payasvini.

✸ *Ram ghat on river Shipra, Ujjain*

✷ *A bathing ghat on river Shipra, Ujjain*

Legends also record the sacredness of Shipra. It is noted in the puranas that ascetics like Narada, Bhrigu, Angiras, Gandharva, Vasu, Aditya, Asvini Kumar, Murutgan, Rudra, and Pitar devoutedly worshipped Shipra.

In the ancient Sanskrit literature also river Shipra has been described or referred to in various contexts, especially in the compositions of Kalidasa, Sri Harsha, Krishnanand, and Banabhatta.

In the month of Kartik, bathing and offering earthen lamps in Shipra is considered very auspicious. Some religious rites are also performed in the river during this month. Several important temples, ghats, samadhis, maths, old houses, and ashrams are located on either banks of the river. For centuries people have been thronging the ghats of the sacred river not only for holy baths but also to perform life-cycle rituals. Some of the most important ghats, shrines, and temples located on the banks of the river are described below.

* Triveni Navagraha Temple: Located on Triveni ghat of the Shipra, the temple is situated away from the old site of Ujjain

town. The temple, dedicated to the nine planets, attracts large crowds on new moon days falling on Saturdays. Swami Silanandaji Maharaj practised austerity in the temple premises.

* Ram ghat: The most important ghat on the Shipra is Ram ghat, where every evening Sandhya *aarti* is performed. Priests worship the river with flowers, incense, sandalwood, and vermillion. Ram ghat is also known due to the presence of the idols of Pishachamukteshwar, Guheshwar, Aruneshwar, Dundeshwar, Damarukeshwar, and Ardhanarishwar. There is also Datta akhara mainly used by the Naga sanyasis during Kumbha mela.

* Nrisimha ghat: This ghat has a temple dedicated to Narasimha, one of the ten incarnations of Vishnu. During Kumbha mela, the ghat is specially used by the Paramahams sadhus.

* Bhartrihari caves and Pir Matsyendranath shrine: Bhartrihari caves lie close to Gadkalika temple on the banks of Shipra. The shrine of Pir Matsyendranath, founder of the Natha sect of Shaivism, also exists here. Since Muslims as well as the followers of Natha sect call their saints 'Pir', the ancient site of Pir Matsyendranath is venerated by both. Excavations at the site have yielded some antiquities dated back to the 6th and 7th centuries BCE.

* Kaliadeh palace: Constructed in 1458 CE during the reign of Mamud Khilji of Malwa, the beautiful palace is located on a small island on the Shipra which has man-made tanks and waterways inside the complex. The palace exudes the illusion that the entire structure is floating on the sacred waters of the

river. It is believed that there was once a majestic sun temple at the site. Avanti Mahatmya of *Skanda Puarana* describes the Sun temple and two tanks, the Surya Kund and the Brahma Kund. People from nearby villages take ritual dip in the Surya kund even today. Remains of the old temple are found scattered all over the area.

* Gandhavati ghat: This is where river Gandhavati joins Shipra. The ghat is known for the location of temples dedicated to Kameshwar, Dudheshwar, Karkateshwar, as well as Bighna Nayak Ganapati. There is also a kund named Anang Kund within the ghat area.

* Kedareshwar temple: Kedareshwar temple is located on the western bank of Shipra, in front of Sunhari ghat. A dharamshala

✷ *Old structures on the banks of Shipra*

with sixty pillars stand near the temple. This is mainly occupied by Kapalika and Aghora sects of Shiva worshippers.

* Chakratirtha: Chakratirtha is located near a burning ghat where one can see the temples of Anandeshwar, Batuka Bhairava and ten-handed Vinayaka.

* Kalabhairava temple: Situated on the bank of Shipra, this temple is well known for tantriks. The temple is said to have been constructed by king Bhadrasen. By the side of the temple complex are the places of Vikrant Bhairava and the cave of Patal Bhairavi.

* Mangalnath temple: Mangalnath temple is situated on the bank of Shipra. It is mentioned in the *Matsya Purana* that this

✷ *Old ghats on the banks of Shipra river*

✷ *A resting place on the bank of river Shipra*

is the birth place of Mars (Mangal). The temple enshrines an image of Shiva in his Mahadeva manifestations.

* Sandipani Ashram: Sandipani ashram is situated very near to Mangalnath temple on the banks of Shipra. The ashram houses two temples; one is dedicated to Krishna, Balaram, and Sudama; and the other is a Shiva temple. Within the precincts of the ashram there is a sacred tank, namely Gomti Kund. It is said that Krishna called all the holy rivers so that his Guru Sandipani would not have to travel to distant places on pilgrimage.

* Siddhavat: Siddhavat, the enormous banyan tree on the banks of Shipra, is worshipped in the form of a temple. This tree has been vested with the same religious sanctity as the Akshayavat in Prayag and Gaya, Vanshivat of Vrindavan, and the Panchavata of Nasik.

Thousands of pilgrims take a dip in the Shipra from the bathing ghats built there. According to one legend, Parvati has performed her penance here. It used to be a place of worship for the followers of the Natha sect. One legend has it that some Mughal rulers had cut off the Banyan tree and covered the site with iron sheets to prevent it from sprouting and growing. But the tree pierced the sheets and grew and flourished.

River Shipra thus plays the role of more than a temple. It has contributed immensely to the birth, evolution, and development of a temple culture in Ujjain. This is also evident from legendary and factual references in the ancient texts and other literary compositions.

Pilgrimages and Eco-Friendly Tourism

The Hindu places of pilgrimage reflect their validity, resilience, and syncretism. They knit together the linguistically diverse Hindu population socially, culturally, and spatially at different integrative levels. Their significance is measured by their capacity to generate and maintain a massive circulation of religious thoughts and pilgrimages.

Pilgrimages are called *tirtha yatras*, a term which means, 'journeys to sacred places'. The term also highlights the importance which rivers have always had in Hindu pilgrimages. Most pilgrimages today are associated in some way or the other with water. Flower, fruits, or money are still thrown into the sacred rivers as an act of worship. Rivers are thus a prominent part of pilgrimages. Water not only washes outwardly, but also represents inner spiritual cleansing. The banks of rivers have been the favourite dwelling places of gods, gurus and sages, and where many Hindu scriptures have been composed.

Pilgrimages are desirable rituals but not obligatory. Journeys to such places where the Supreme spirit is believed to be manifest in temples, sacred rivers, coasts, or mountains, are considered to be very auspicious and karmically rewarding. Many pilgrimages are undertaken to acquire good karma, to perform certain rituals for the deceased ancestors (often considered obligatory) or because of a festival.

Looking at the importance, essential features, and characteristics of pilgrimages and the role of a sacred river in those, Shipra river valley in Ujjain has been an ideal place for pilgrimages from ancient times. Pilgrimage to the holy sites located in the Shipra valley is known as one form of *karma*, which brings emancipation from worldly sufferings.

Legend has it that Ujjain is one of the Saptapuris (the seven holy cities) of India that grants *moksha* (liberation from the cycle of births and deaths). Apart from this, the *yatra* has also been considered a carrier of mankind across the sea of sufferings, the Bhav Sagar. Before undertaking a pilgrimage, the pilgrims have to prepare themselves for the task. The journeys are undertaken through different methods; through an organised tour, or by public transport, or on foot. Individuals have to endure both mental and physical challenges, such as plain discomfort, uncomfortable surroundings, theft, shortage of food, and so on. However, with improved means of transport, pilgrimages have become easier. Pilgrimages are now undertaken by children, young people, and the elderly. There is always a desire to return home doubly blessed and amply rewarded, a basic change in attitude towards the *yatra*.

However, the facilities available currently for pilgrimages to shrines located on the Shipra river valley are grossly inadequate. To promote eco-friendly tourism and pilgrimage, several measures need to be taken by the authorities.

The pilgrims/tourists visiting religious shrines and other places of interest in Ujjain and the Malwa region includes the rich, upper/lower middle class, as well as poor people. The rich people generally travel by their own vehicles. They do not face any problem on the way because they can afford to pay high prices for their travel, food, and accommodation. The upper/lower middle class pilgrims/tourists generally undertake pilgrimages along with sightseeing. Their travels are arranged by private travel agencies or Madhya Pradesh State Tourism Development Corporation. These tours offer wide choice of accommodation including exotic log huts and comfortable lodges in luxury hotels and colonial bungalows. Strategically located, every unit has been built with the comfort of visitors in mind. Aesthetically designed and complete with all modern amenities, the main focus is on care and comfort.

The worst sufferers are the poor pilgrims and travellers on foot. The poor pilgrims undertake their *yatra* by public conveyance or by private buses under a caretaker who takes a commission. Travellers on foot generally include *sanyasi*s (hermits), itinerant vagabonds, wandering minstrels, and low caste people from the neighbouring states of Uttar Pradesh, Rajasthan, Gujarat, and Maharashtra.

While developing eco-friendly tourism and promoting pilgrimage to the sacred shrines in Ujjain, the problems of the poor pilgrims should be given due consideration.

* The accommodation facilities available in various *dharamshalas*, tourist bungalows, hotels, and rest houses are not enough to meet the growing needs of pilgrims and tourists. The government tourist hotels/tourist bungalows, private lodges/hotels, PWD inspection houses, and other guest houses located at important halting places on the way to Ujjain provide accommodation. The number of travellers during the yatra season, however, rises to such an extent that the accommodation facilities available are not enough to meet their needs, especially poor pilgrims and travellers on foot.

* The boarding and lodging charges are increased substantially during the pilgrimage season. The poor pilgrims are unable to meet the huge expenditures on lodging. Sometimes they spend their time either in the buses or in nearby homes where one or two rooms are spared for their overnight stay on payment of nominal charges.

* During season pilgrims generally arrive from distant places and neighbouring states such as Uttar Pradesh, Rajasthan, Gujarat, and Maharashtra. Those coming from other states have different food habits. They face lot of difficulties because they do not get suitable food.

To promote eco-friendly tourism and pilgrimage in Ujjain, the following steps may be taken.

* The number of package tours organised by the state tourism may be increased during pilgrimage season.

* Tourist bungalows, traveller's lodges, *dharamshalas*, hotels, PWD inspection bungalows and other rest houses or private lodging houses or hotels are not within the reach of poor pilgrims. It will be in their interest if the government constructs dormitories which will ease the tension of the poor travellers, especially during nights.

* Keeping in view the interests of pilgrims, food stalls may be set up at appropriate halting stations where food suitable to them is made available during the pilgrimage season.

* During the pilgrimage season hotels hike their charges. This causes undue stress on the pilgrims. To promote eco-friendly tourism, this practice should be discontinued forthwith. Keeping the plight of the pilgrims in view the Mahakaleshwar temple administration provides the following facilities to the pilgrims:
    * It maintains a large *dharmashala* near the temple. Apart from lodging, boarding facilities are also available here. It runs a free annakhetra for the pilgrims. Pilgrims not staying at Mahakaleshwar *dharmashala* can also avail of this facility.
    * For puja and *abhishek* a special chamber is available near the *garbhagriha* of the temple.
    * Cloak room and toilet facilities are also available behind the temple complex.
    * The temple administration has also made special arrangements for abhishek for the pilgrims. Those who register with them can watch the abhishek.

* Even prasad (laddoo prasad and Bhasma Aarti prasad with pancha mewa) are available in packets in the temple premises.

If such facilities are provided by other temples in Ujjain also, the visiting pilgrims will be benefitted to a great extent.

River Shipra gets polluted as a large number of pilgrims take bath in it on auspicious occasions or religious festivals or before entering the temple. Moreover, the local population also pollutes the water of the sacred river by throwing garbage and by directing dirty water into the river. The local administration should take appropriate steps to educate people to refrain from such unhealthy and inauspicious activities.

Pilgrimages unite people from different regions of the country. They all move together which generates a strong spiritual link. It is indeed no naïve assumption that the world might be a happier place if more people promote inter-cultural communication and fundamental affinity among them, irrespective of race, community, class, colour, or creed.

Appendices

Appendix 1

Eighty-four Mahadevas in Ujjain

Sl No.	Name of Mahadeva	Location
1.	Agastheswar	Behind Harsiddhi temple complex
2.	Guheshwar	Ramghat, on the bank of river Shipra
3.	Dundeshwar	Ram Sidhi (Ramghat) on the bank of river Shipra
4.	Damrukeshar	Ram Sidhi (Ramghat) on the bank of river Shipra
5.	Anadikalpeshwar	Mahakaleshwar temple complex
6.	Swarnajaleshwar	Ram Sidhi (Ramghat) on the bank of river Shipra
7.	Trivishtapeshwar	Mahakaleshwar temple complex
8.	Kapaleshwar	Anantapeth
9.	Swargadwareshwar	Nalia Bakhal
10.	Kakotishwar	Harsiddhi temple complex

11.	Siddheshwar	Siddhanath
12.	Lokapaleshwar	Harsiddhi temple complex
13.	Kameshwar	Gandhavati ghat on the bank of river Shipra
14.	Kutumbeshwar	Singhpuri
15.	Indradhumneshwar	Modi-ki-gali
16.	Ishaneshwar	Modi-ki-gali
17.	Apsareshwar	Patni Bazar, on the northern side of Modi-ki-gali.
18.	Kalkaleshwar	Modi-ki-gali
19.	Nagchandreshwar	Patni Bazar, Nagnath-ki-gali
20.	Pratihareshwar	On the eastern door of Nagchandreshwar
21.	Kukkuteshwar	Gandhavati Ghat on the bank of river Shipra
22.	Karketeshwar	Khatikwada
23.	Meghnadeshwar	Chhota Sarafa
24.	Mahalayeshwar	Khatriwada
25.	Mukteshwar	Khatriwada
26.	Someshwar	Anantapeth
27.	Anarkeshwar	Makoria Am-Indira Nagar
28.	Jateshwar	Gayakotha
29.	Rameshwar	Near Sati Darwaja
30.	Chavaneshwar	Near Idgah
31.	Khandeshwar	Khilchipur
32.	Pattaneshwar	Khilchipur
33.	Anandeshwar	Electric crematorium
34.	Kanthadeshwar	Near Siddhanath
35.	Indreshwar	Anantapeth
36.	Markandeshwar	Near Ram Janardan temple
37.	Shiveshwar	In Ram Janardan temple complex
38.	Kusumeshwar	In Ram Janardan temple complex
39.	Akrureshwar	In Ram Janardan temple complex
40.	Kundeshwar	Gomti Kund
41.	Lumpeshwar	Near Khedapati Hanuman temple, Bhairavgarh
42.	Gangeshwar	Khargata Sangam (Mangalnath ghat)

43.	Angarkeshwar	In Mangalnath temple complex
44.	Uttareshwar	In Mangalnath temple complex
45.	Trilochaneshwar	Ramaji Jat ki gali, Namdarpura
46.	Veereshwar	Dani Darwaja, near Satyanarayan temple on Dhaba road
47.	Nripureshwar	Dabri pitha gali
48.	Abhayeshwar	Dani Darwaja
49.	Prithukeshwar	In Kedareshwar temple on the chhota pool
50.	Sthavareshwar	Nai peth
51.	Shuleshwar	Khatikwada
52.	Omkareshwar	Khatikwada
53.	Vishveshwar	Khatikwada
54.	Kantheshwar	Piplinaka
55.	Singheshwar	Near Chintaman Ganesha temple complex
56.	Revanteshwar	Kartik Chowk
57.	Ghanteshwar	Kartik Chowk
58.	Prayageshwar	Rajamal-ka-ghat
59.	Siddheshwar	Khatriwada
60.	Matangeshwar	Pinjar-wadi
61.	Saubhagyeshwar	Patni Bazar, Saubhagyeshwar ki gali
62.	Rupeshwar	Singhpuri
63.	Dhanusahatreshwar	Girinari Hanuman
64.	Pashupateshwar	Jansapura
65.	Brahmeshwar	Khatikwada
66.	Jalpeshwar	On the way to Ranjit Hanuman
67.	Kedareshwar	In front of Sunherighat
68.	Pishachamukteshwar	Ramghat on the bank of the river Shipra
69.	Sangameshwar	In front of Jayramdas Sanehiram's garden, behind Virat Hanuman
70.	Durdhareshwar	Gandhavati ghat on the bank of river Shipra
71.	Prayageshwar	Near Harsiddhi temple complex
72.	Chandradityeshwar	In Mahakaleshwar temple complex
73.	Karbheshwar	Near Kalabhairava temple complex

74.	Rajsthaleshwar	Bhagshipura
75.	Badleshwar	In Siddhavat complex near Bhairavgarh
76.	Aruneshwar	Below Ram Sidhi at Ramghat on the bank of river Shipra
77.	Pushpadanteshwar	Singhpuri
78.	Abimukteshwar	Singhpuri
79.	Hanumakteshwar	Near Gadkalika temple complex
80.	Swapneshwar	In Mahakaleshwar temple complex
81.	Pingleshwar	In village Pingleshwar
82.	Kayavarohaneshwar	In village Karohan
83.	Billeshwar	In village Amodiya
84.	Durdureshwar	In village Jayathal

Appendix II

Twelve *Jyotirlingas* in India

Sl No.	Name of the Jyotirlinga	Location
1.	Somnath	Saurashtra
2.	Mallikarjuna	Sri Saila
3.	Mahakaleshwar	Ujjain
4.	Omkareshwar	Vindhyachal
5.	Kedarnath	Himalaya
6.	Bhimshankar	Dakini Kshetra
7.	Vishwanath	Varanasi
8.	Trambakeshwar	Gautami Tata (Nasik)
9.	Nageshwar	Dwarka
10.	Vaidyanath	Parali
11.	Rameshwar	Setubandhana
12.	Ghrishameshwar	Shivalaya (Ellora)

Acknowledgements

This book contains the data collected through field investigations and other sources, and used in a research project report submitted to the Indian Council of Historical Research (ICHR), Ministry of Human Resource Development, New Delhi. I am grateful to ICHR for kindly sponsoring my research project on the temple culture of Ujjain during 2010–11. I am also thankful to the Indian Archaeological Society, New Delhi, which, as the affiliating institution for the project, extended all possible help and cooperation.

The book is intended to provide important and helpful information to the English-knowing inter-state visitors, pilgrims and foreign tourists who may be interested to have an idea of the temple culture of Ujjain before their visits to this age-old city of temples.

Most of the photographs included in the book were taken during the field investigations. Some important photographs were, however, made available by the M.P. Tourism Office, Bhopal, Shri Mahakaleshwar Mandir Prabandh Samiti, Ujjain, and Dr Mamta Pandey of the M.P. Tourism Office, New Delhi. I would like to extend my warmest gratitude to them.

I have no words to express my gratitude to Niyogi Books for their unstinted assistance and co-operation throughout the production process of this book.

M.K. Pal
New Delhi

Glossary

Abhisheka	Pouring of libations on the image of the deity, amidst the chanting of mantras. Usually, offerings such as milk, yogurt, ghee, honey, Panchamrita, sesame oil, rosewater, and sandalwood paste may be poured among other offerings.
Akhanda jyoti	A lamp which burns continuously
Akhara	A place with facilities for board, lodging, and education
Amavasya	The last day of the dark half of a month
Amrita	Nectar, the drink of the gods
Amrita sambhava	One who generates nectar
Antarala	Vestibule
Anuchara	Attendant
Apsaras	Extremely beautiful, youthful, and elegant supernatural female beings superb in the art of dancing
Aarati	A religious ritual of worship, a part of puja, in which light from wicks soaked in ghee or camphor is offered to the diety
Akhanda jyoti	Continuously burning lamp
Ashram	Hermitage, a reclusary, for monks
Ashtadhatu	The eight metals, namely gold, silver, copper, brass, tin, lead, iron, and bell-metal
Bel	The wood-apple *Aeglemarmelos*
Bhiksha	Holy offerings of food
Bilva patra	The leaf of wood-apple *Aeglemarmelos*
Brahmana/Brahmin	The highest ranking of the four varnas, the others being kshatriya, vaishya and sudra.

Chaturthi	The fourth lunar day
Chintaharan	Remover of worries
Damaru	A tabor or small drum in the shape of an hour glass
Darshan	Paying visit (generally to a temple)
Deepasthambha	Pillar with several lines of lamps, usually made of stone
Deepavali (Diwali)	Festival of lights which falls on the 15th day of the dark half of the month of Kartik (October–November)
Devasthan	Abode of the gods
Dewan	A minister
Dharmashala	Shelter for pilgrims and devotees
Ekadashi	The eleventh day in the fortnight of a lunar month
Ganga	The most sacred river of Hindus, worshipped as a goddess
Garbhagriha	Sanctum sanctorum, the inner room in a temple where the idol is situated
Ghat	Bathing place on the bank of a river
Gora	White
Govardhandhari	One who holds the mountain Govardhan – Lord Krishna
Graha	Planet
Halahala	A very deadly poison
Havan	Ritual of making offerings into a consecrated fire
Japa	The silent repetition or muttering of a prayer
Jvarghani	Destroyer of fever
Kala	Black
Kapala	Skull
Karka	The sign of Zodiac Cancer
Karma	Action, work or deed. It also refers to the principle of causality where intent and actions of an individual influence the future of that individual.
Katimekhla	A waist band
Kativastra	Cloth worn around the loin
Keyura	An armlet or a bracelet worn on the upper arm
Kshirsagar	Ocean of milk
Kulaguru	Spiritual guide of a family or clan
Kumbha	Pitcher

Kund	Pool
Kundala	A large ear ring, a pendant
Kundali	Girdle of the playful king of the serpents
Lingam	Phallus
Mahi Valaya	Girdle of serpent
Mandapam	A platform used to conduct religious or social ceremonies
Mandir	Temple
Matha	A hermitage, an abbey
Mela	Fair
Moksha	Eternal liberation from the cycle of births and deaths
Mrityulok	The land of mortals – the Earth
Mrityunjaya	One who has conquered death
Mundamala	A garland of severed heads
Nag	Serpent
Naivedya	Offerings made to a deity, oblation
Navagrahas	The nine planets on which astronomical calculations are based
Navaratna	Literally, the nine gems. The mention here is to the nine greatest poets and scholars of that time in the court of Emperor Vikramaditya.
Navaratri	The first nine days of the bright half of Aswin or Chaitra
Neem	The margosa tree (*Azadirachta indica*)
Pandit	A wise and learned man
Papaghani / Papanashini	Destroyer of all sins
Parva	Festival
Patala	The world beneath
Pipal	The holy fig tree (*Ficus religiosa*)
Pitha	An altar, pedestal
Pradakshinapath	Circumambulatory passage along which devotees take rounds around the sanctum sanctorum
Pradosh	Sunset, evening
Pratirupa	Image
Puja	Worship, performance of rituals

Puranas	Ancient Hindu texts eulogising various deities, primarily Brahma, Vishnu, and Shiva, through divine stories
Rishi	Seer
Sabhagriha	A congregation hall
Sadhu	A hermit, a mendicant
Samadhi	A higher level of concentrated meditation. Also means to experience 'oneness with the universe', or death
Samudramanthan	Churning of the ocean
Sanad	A grant, a charter
Saptamatrikas	Seven mother goddesses
Shahi	Royal
Sakshi	Evidence
Shakti	Literally, power. Also Devi Parvati, Shiva's consort
Sarpahara	A serpent in the form of a necklace
Savari	Procession
Sehra	Bridegroom's floral crown
Shikhara	Cupola, a small dome forming part of the roof
Shivalingam	Symbolic phallus of Shiva
Shivaratri	A Hindu festival celebrated every year on the 13th night of Phalgun month of the Hindu calendar in reverence of Lord Shiva
Shraddha	Last rites for departed souls
Skanda Purana	Largest of 18 puranas, describing the activities of Lord Skanda or Karthikeya, son of Shiva and Parvati.
Swayambhu	Self-manifested and drawing power from itself
Tithi	Lunar day or night as set by the motions and positions of the stars, moon, and the planets
Triratha	Schema of hindu temples with three facets. Other schemas are pancharatha, saptaratha, and navaratha (5, 7, and 9 facets, respectively)
Trishula	The trident, the weapon of Shiva
Tulsi	The holy basil plant
Ugra	Ferocious
Urusrnga	Mini spire, pointed structure in the form of a tall cone or pyramid
Uttaravahini	That which flows to the north
Vaikuntha	Abode of Lord Mahavishnu

Valaya	Bracelet
Vata	Indian fig tree, the banyan tree
Yatra	Pilgrimage. Literally, journey.
Yoga	Profound meditation
Yogini	A female ascetic

Bibliography

Ali, Raman. 2002. *Temples of Madhya Pradesh: The Paramara Art*. New Delhi: Sundeep Prakashan.

Bezbaruah, M.P. (Ch ed.). 2003. *Fairs and Festivals of India*, Vol. IV. New Delhi: Gyan Publishing House.

Bhardwaj, S.M. 1973. *Hindu Places of Pilgrimage in India: A Study in Cultural Geography*. California: University of California Press.

Catalogue of Coins of Ancient India in the British Museum, London, 1936, Plate XI, No. 2 (Ujjain), p. 85.

Dey, Upendra Nath. 1965. *Medieval Malwa: A Political and Cultural History, 1401–1562*. New Delhi: Munshiram Manoharlal.

Dvivedi, Bhavarlal. 2004. *Avantika Mahatmya* (in Hindi). Ujjain: Jay Sri Krishna Bhakti Bhandar.

GoI. *The Temples of India*. 1964. Department of Tourism, Government of India.

Jain, Kailash Chand. 1972. *Malwa through the Ages from the Earliest Times to 1305 A.D.* Delhi: Motilal Banarsidass.

Kramrisch, Stella. 1976. *The Hindu Temple II*. Delhi: Motilal Banarsidass.

Law, B.C. 1954. *Historical Geography of Ancient India*. Paris: Societe Asiatique de Paris.

Meister, Michael W., M.A. Dhaky, Krishna Deva (eds). 1988. *Encyclopedia of Indian Temple Architecture*. Delhi: American Institute of Indian Studies, Oxford University Press.

Patil, D.R. 1952. *The Cultural Heritage of Madhya Bharat*. Gwalior: Department of Archaeology, Government of Madhya Bharat.

Puri, B.N. 1966. *Cities of Ancient India*. Meerut: Meenakshi Prakashan.

Ramlal, Kawal. 1984. *Prachin Malwa me Mandir Vastukala* (in Hindi). New Delhi: Swati Publications.

Sarma, I.K. 1982. *The Development of Early Saiva Art and Architecture*. New Delhi: Sundeep Prakashan.

Sen, B.C. 1942. *Some Historical Aspects of the Inscriptions of Bengal*. Calcutta: University of Calcutta.

Seth, K.N. 1978. *The Growth of the Paramara Power in Malwa*. Bhopal: Progress Publishers.

Sharma, B.N. 1978. *Festivals of India*. New Delhi: Abhinav Publications.

Sharma, R.K. 1979. *Art of the Paramaras of Malwa*. Delhi: Agamkala Prakashan.

Shastri, Shri Brahmashankar, *Meghadutam*, Chowkhamba Sanskrit Series Office, P.O. Box 8, Varanasi, 1959.

Shri Mahakaleshwar Mandir Prabandh Samiti. 2006. *Jyotirlinga Shri Mahakaleshwara*. Ujjain: Shri Mahakaleshwar Mandir Prabandh Samiti.

Sircar, D.C. 1969. *Ancient Malwa and the Vikramaditya Tradition*. New Delhi: Munshiram Manoharlal.

Wheeler, Sir Mortimer. 1968. *The Indus Civilization*, Cambridge University Press, p. 142.

Booklets and leaflets issued by Madhya Pradesh Tourism Development Corporation Ltd., various Websites. M.P. Tourism office, New Delhi.

Index